Contents

Introduction – Why Small Businesses Fail ..11

Interesting Statistics..14

6 Keys to Success as a Small Business Owner.......15

Why Do Small Businesses Fail? 17

Startups Are Especially Vulnerable......................18

Chapter 1 - Assessing the Problems...........20

9 Reasons Small Retail Businesses Fail................21

Neglect..22

Tunnel Vision..23

Cash Flow Issue..23

Ever Increasing Overhead Cost 24

Leadership Issues 27

Customer Experience.....................................29

Overexpansion..33

Theft, Fraud & Other Crimes 35

Competition..37

Learning from Failure..38

SWOT Analysis...43

ID The Real Problem...45

Questions to Consider about Sales 46

Questions to Consider about Your Products or Services 47

Questions to Consider about Employees 48

Questions to Consider about Profits & Losses 49

Chapter 2 – Financial Challenges 51

Funding Sources 52

Investors and Partners 55

Investors 56

Partners 58

Three Types of Partnerships 58

Working Partner 58

Equal Partners 60

Multiple Partners With One Key Operating Person 64

5 Keys to Successful Partnerships 67

Crowdfunding 69

Two Approaches to Crowdfunding 70

Success Tips for Crowdfunding 73

Chapter 3 – Getting a Bank Loan 77

Choosing the Right Bank 78

SMALL BUSINESS 911

Learn to Solve Financing, Negative Cash Flow, Staffing, Theft, Partnership & Legal Issues

Secrets of Marketing & Branding While lowering Overhead cost & Boost Profit

By

Shabbir Hossain

Copyrighted Material

Copyright © 2022 – **CSB Academy Publishing Company**

All Rights Reserved.

Without limiting the rights under the copyright laws, no part of this publication may be reproduced, stored in or introduced into a retrieval system, or transmitted, in any form or by any means (electronic, mechanical, photocopying, recording or otherwise), without the prior written consent of the publisher of this book.

CSB Academy Publishing Company publishes its books and guides in a variety of electronic and print formats, Some content that appears in print may not be available in electronic format, and vice versa.

CSB ACADEMY PUBLISHING COMPANY.

COVER DESIGN BY

STEPHANIE MARTIN

FIRST EDITION

Different Types of Loans.................................80

    What is an SBA Loan?.................................80

    Conventional Business Loan..........................81

Three Types of Capital 81

Loan Package & Documentation 83

Chapter 4 – Legal Matters.........................87

Bulletproof Bookkeeping..................................88

Accounting Software.......................................90

Keeping Good Records 92

Small Business Taxes......................................93

    Tax Deductions: What Can I Write Off? 94

    What can I deduct? 95

    Cost of Goods Sold 96

    Capital Expenses..97

    Other Types of Business Expenses* 98

Business Structures 99

    Types of Businesses...................................100

    Registering an LLC....................................102

Business Insurance Options 103

Chapter 5 – A Solid Business Plan.............108

What is a Professional Business Plan?................109

How to Write a Business Plan 110

What Goes Inside Your Business Plan 110

   Cover letter 111

   9 Parts of a Business Plan............................113

SMART Goals 118

   Creating a Specific Goal...............................121

   Creating a Measurable Goal 122

   Creating an Achievable Goal.........................122

   Creating a Relevant Goal 123

   Creating a Timely Goal 124

Chapter 6 – Excellent Employees 126

10 Steps to Successful Staffing 128

   How to Find the Right Staff..........................128

   Asking the Right Interview Questions 132

   Providing Proper Training.............................137

   Employee Appearance 139

   Motivating & Empowering Your Staff 140

   Teaching Them Marketing 101.......................141

   Rewarding Good Behavior.............................142

   How to Discipline Bad Behavior 143

   Goal-Oriented Incentives..............................144

Regular Employee Meetings & Coaching 146

Chapter 7 – Selling Secrets: Five Proven Ways to Increase Sales 148

1 - Product Merchandising & Pricing 149

    A Tale of 3 Stores 150

    Three-month check-up 154

2 - Staff 156

3 - Marketing & Promotions 157

    4 Local Area Promotion Ideas 158

4 - Streamlining Costs & Expenses 162

5 - Minimizing Theft & Errors 164

    Steps to Defer External Theft 165

    Preventing Vendor Theft 166

    Preventing Internal Theft 166

    Fostering Loyalty 168

4 Steps to Boost Sales 25% in 60 Days 169

    1. Product Refresh 169

    2. Employee Pep Talk 171

    3. Promotions 171

    4. Reducing Costs 172

How did you do? 173

Chapter 8 – Selling Online 175

Do I Need a Website?...176

But Isn't a Website Expensive?......................177

Isn't Building a Website Hard?......................179

But I Don't Have the Patience! *180*

How to Take Payments on a Website.................181

Other Options 185

Facebook Marketplace......................................186

Etsy..187

Selling at Local Stores.......................................188

Other Local Options 190

Chapter 9 – Profit: Competitive Analysis, Creative Pricing, & Forecasting 193

Competitive Analysis...193

Creative Pricing Strategy 195

Understanding Profit: Penny Profit, Profit Margin, and Markup..197

Penny Profit..197

Profit Margin 198

Markup 199

Business Forecasting..200

Chapter 10 – Branding & Marketing 203

The 5 Ps of Marketing 204

Your Target Market...205

What Is Branding?...209

Brand Identity..210

Your Logo..213

Low-Cost Marketing 215

Should I Offer Discounts and Sales?....................217

Location, Visibility, & Street Traffic 219

Your Social Media Presence...............................221

Chapter 11 – Social Media Marketing 223

Using Facebook for Your Business......................225

Quick FB Tips:..226

Using Facebook to Boost Sales 228

Should I Use Facebook Ads? 229

Using Instagram for Your Business.....................231

Tip: Links in Instagram 232

How Do I Choose Hashtags? 234

Should I Use Instagram Ads?.........................235

Using Pinterest for Your Business......................236

Getting Started on Pinterest..........................239

    How to Create Good Pins 240

    Do I use hashtags on Pinterest posts? 241

    Should I Use Pinterest Ads? 243

Using Twitter for Your Business 243

    Hashtags on Twitter 245

    Should I Use Twitter Ads? 246

    How Often Should I Post? 247

    Overwhelmed by Posting? 248

What to Post on Social Media 249

Utilizing Email 253

Chapter 12 – Staying Motivated 256

Free Resources, Help, & Advice 257

7 Small Business Associations 258

Important Issues 262

    Work/Life Balance 262

    Focus/Looking Ahead 263

    Remember to Outsource 264

INTRODUCTION – WHY SMALL BUSINESSES FAIL

Over the past 26 years, I have started, bought and or sold several small businesses in a variety of categories: gas stations, fast food, restaurants, pizza delivery, liquor store, wholesale warehouse and even book publishing.

Success often comes after failure. If you have a good vision and a strong work ethic, take it from me—you can make it in business. But you must stay determined, keep going, and also know when to let go of an idea that's not working in order to try something new.

SUCCESS OFTEN COMES AFTER FAILURE.

I wish someone would have told me this when I first began my journey as an idealistic young man who came to America to study business. When I graduated from the University of South Alabama in 1994, I dreamed of having my own successful company one day. Through hard work, failure, success, and continual learning, I think I have done okay.

However, I had many years of experience to go through before that dream came true—years of ups and downs, of lean times, of hard lessons, of figuring out what worked and what didn't. Many were things I could never have learned in my business classes, things that I had to learn in the hard school of life.

I have been involved in various small businesses for little over two decades now. As a sort of passion project, I also help other gas station owners thrive. You may have heard of my podcast on gasstationbusiness101.com. There are a lot of free resources and business document templates, as well as advice from my experience.

At any rate, I have learned firsthand many of the reasons that small businesses fail, things that can go wrong, things we can overlook, common challenges, and a variety of struggles.

Why do I do it? Why have I opened so many businesses over the years? Because I love business. I enjoy trying new things to see what succeeds or fails. I like finding ways to connect with customers, seeing what attracts people to a product or a business. I am always coming up with new ideas to try, ways to test the market, ways to improve my products and my businesses.

Sadly, many small business owners quit after their first or second failed attempt at a business. But I don't think of failure as failure. I think of it as a learning opportunity. And I believe that if you have a good vision and a strong work ethic, you can make it. So I wrote this book to support you, my fellow small business owner, in your journey to success.

You obviously picked up this book because there's something in your business that needs improvement. Let me tell you, it's not impossible. There are many good resources here to assist you along the way. I'm here to help you on your journey.

So first let's look at the world of small businesses, why they are important, and why they struggle.

Interesting Statistics

If you are a small business owner, you're in good company. As of April 2020, the 31.7 million small businesses in the United States accounted for 99.9% of all businesses in the country (sba.gov).

You are incredibly important to this nation's economy. Small businesses like yours employed 47.1% of the entire country's workforce—that's 60.6 million people employed by small businesses.

Small businesses employ 47.1% of the U.S. workforce

Nearly 9 million of those employees work in health care and social assistance; 8.5 million work in the accommodation and food services industry; 5.5 million work in retail, and 5.3 million work in construction (sba.gov).

But only about half of all small businesses will make it to their 5-year anniversary. You need more than a dream or personal drive to have a successful small business.

6 Keys to Success as a Small Business Owner

Owning your own business requires several facets in order to succeed. Aside from flexibility, a desire to grow, a willingness to change and work hard, there are six key components that are required:

1. First, you must practice **analytical thinking**. Asking yourself (or other people) why something fails or succeeds. How to make it better. Thinking of ways to fix it or try something new. This can be as simple as changing a store display to get more attention on a product or thinking of ways to boost sales on your slowest day of the week. You don't

need to reinvent the wheel, you just have to make sure it is running like a well-oiled wheel, smooth and steady.

2. You must also be **organized**. If you're running the show, you need to know when your supplies are getting low, how much you paid your supplier and when, and keep your employees' information safe and secure.

3. You must keep **detailed records** of everything: inventory, finances, employee performance and hours, profits and loss. It will teach you where your problem areas are and also cover you in the event of an audit. It will enhance performance and provide protection.

4. You must be aware of your **competition**. Learn from them. What are they doing well? Mimic that. Where are they lacking? Knock it out of the park, and you'll get some of their business.

5. Every small business owner will tell you that working for yourself is harder than working for someone else. It is more demanding and challenging and time-consuming than punching

a clock. Be prepared to make **personal sacrifices** when you are first establishing your business. But maintain work/life balance. Otherwise, what is it for?

6. **Customer service** needs to be a top priority to you. If you provide good service to your customers, you'll gain their loyalty and retain their business so that the business can grow in the long term.

Why Do Small Businesses Fail?

When you read reports and articles about why small businesses fail, these three things are generally at the top of the list:

No market/product not needed: In other words, nobody was interested in their product. It didn't solve a need. More research ahead of time is key to preventing this major mistake.

Ran out of cash: Startups are especially susceptible to this, as starting a business requires so many first-time costs up front. It's best to estimate that your startup fees will be double what you expect. It never hurts to be prepared, but it can be devastating not to be.

Team issues: Having the right people in the right positions is a critical part of success in small businesses. Honestly assessing your own skill set and those of your team is key.

Other common reasons included poor pricing, not having a user-friendly product, not having a good business plan, poor marketing, and insufficient communication with customers (not getting their input or taking it to heart).

Other less common problems that are still common are being outdone by their competition, a lack of passion, insufficient work-life balance, legal problems, and poor timing in the market.

STARTUPS ARE ESPECIALLY VULNERABLE

The first few years of your small business are its most vulnerable time. According to the U.S. Small Business Administration:

- 20% of small businesses fail in their first year

- 50% bite the bullet after five years

- Only 33% make it to 10 years or longer

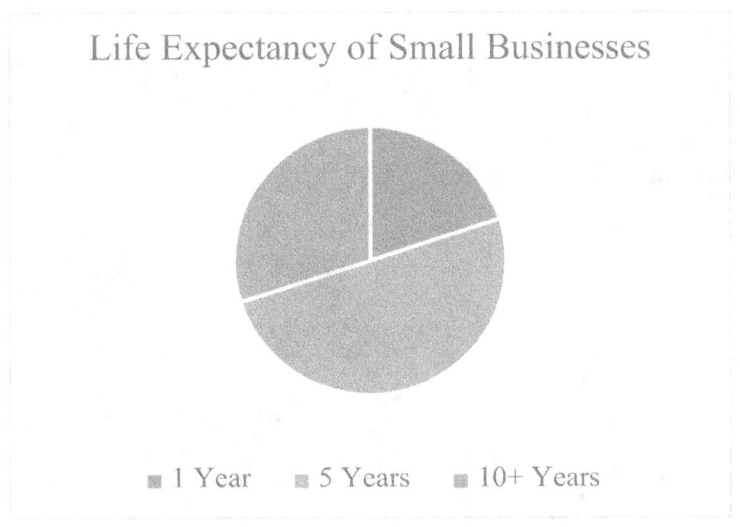

Source: Small Business Administration

As you can see, only half of all small businesses will last past the 5-year mark. But I'm sure that with more planning, a better grip on your finances, and working out some of your specific pain points and weak areas, you can be in the one-third that lasts 10 years or more.

Chapter 1 - Assessing the Problems

So what are you doing wrong, exactly? Sometimes it's hard to tell.

It's a common problem. You are so close to your business that it's hard to be objective, to see things as they really are. It's easy to get tunnel vision—where you cannot see the big picture because you are too close to it or you're focused only on one thing. This makes it hard to see your business from the outside or to see your problems accurately.

You're not alone. But picking up this book is a positive step to help gain some perspective.

Whether your business is retail or not, keep reading. We are going to talk about a lot of general issues with small businesses. But first I would like to share from my experience owning stores, restaurants, and gas stations for the past 25+ years. Read on to learn my top 9 reasons that small retail businesses fail.

9 Reasons Small Retail Businesses Fail

To understand retail sales, you have to recognize the problems first. All business owners know how important it is to increase sales, and I am sure most of you do want to increase sales. But why do you then still fail to achieve the sales target?

What is it that differentiates your business from your competitor, who is essentially selling the same merchandise? Surely, there are many factors involved but let's take a look at some of the problems that may be affecting your retail sales. Keep in mind that all of these may not apply to your business, but it is a good idea to keep a note of the ones that you think do affect your business. Ready? Let's dive in.

Neglect

Setting up any business requires a visionary entrepreneur, but forming a company is only part of the challenge, and the rest lies in continuous and consistent direction and involvement from the leadership. Without that, a company can soon lose its direction and fail to sustain itself in the face of new problems and challenges. For a company to boost its sales, it's important to continuously review, maintain, and develop it to keep it at its peak performance.

At no point can a company be neglected and still hope to run profitably. External forces that affect a company's bottom line are forever changing, and any neglect can throw a retail sales business off. As an owner, whether it's a small shop, big boutique, or a gas station, you need to take notice of the changing factors and change along with them to keep the business up to date and to thrive.

Tunnel Vision

When you work IN your business every day, it is hard to look at it from a distance and analyze problems. Essentially, that is what we call tunnel vision. You are so consumed in your everyday operation that you can't figure out what it is that you or your employees are doing wrong, or not doing at all.

You need an outside perspective in your business. It also helps to ask your customers what they want to see in your business or what areas need improvement. Listen to them and write it down.

Cash Flow Issue

Cash is King! Cash is also an important part of your business growth, and while a company may have started with a minimum of financial capital, there may reach a point when additional money is required to grow or to buy additional inventory or to do some much-needed upgrades. If additional funds are not available, it could be difficult for a business to meet its day-to-day obligations which can hamper your ability to increase sales.

Mastering the art of managing money is one of the key resources of a business that helps it keep within its limits and maximize the use of its available funds. Any company that goes over the limit in debt fails to see the light of day. Many small retail stores don't follow proper accounting practices which could be a big dent in their time and efforts around tax filing season or when they go to get a loan.

Having your business finances in order, whether yourself or through a professional accountant, ensures that you keep track of your money and understand how much the business is making in profits. Making projections for the future becomes easier when you have everything organized in accounting software and not on paper.

Ever Increasing Overhead Cost

As important as it is to study success, the same is true of failure. It points out the glitches in the system, which can lead to success if they are overcome. No process is efficient from the beginning, but it is made so with continuous improvements and developments, which is all due to the effort of a business's leadership. When starting a new business, most people overlook failures and focus only on making money.

Money can be made only when you look at potential problems and know how to overcome them. Business growth is a learning process, but the better prepared you are, the farther you will go. As a business owner, your primary focus should be to efficiently run your business with the best resources available to you and make it a lean, mean machine so everyone knows the process and can repeat the same result every time. Money is a byproduct of success, so if you run your business effectively, the money will come. Sounds easy I know but it is not hard to do.

The retail sales industry is an evolving and rapidly changing industry with technology stepping in to shape the nature of things for good. How well you adapt to each coming change defines your ability to succeed in the retail world. Success and profits come only after you are able to provide your customer with a valuable experience.

Businesses that work on developing good customer experiences through their sales and after sale services, and by making the process smooth, find it easier to discover their path to growth. That's because your customer should be your priority and not your business—this attitude is what makes your business success. Considering them as an integral part of your business is what will allow you to continuously find and nurture new opportunities to provide a better experience.

> YOUR CUSTOMER SHOULD BE YOUR PRIORITY, NOT YOUR BUSINESS.

With the rapid changes in the business world, the cost of doing business is going up too, and that is one uphill battle that is harder to win. From labor cost to utility bills, everything is going up. But your profit margin is not going up nor is your sales volume. Lately, some of us in retail are faced with the new cost of technology like EMV updates. Most cash registers and ATMs are now required to be upgraded to handle the Chip-based credit cards. This is a huge upfront cost, and in some businesses, it can cost as much as $20,000 to comply with the new guidelines.

Leadership Issues

Management problems are real issues, and they can destroy a company. While an entrepreneur may be effective at starting a business from a mere idea, they may not be ready to face the management problems associated with it.

If you don't have good people on your team, if you don't train them properly, if you don't coach them often, if you don't pay them enough or aren't willing to treat people the right way, then chances are, your company will suffer.

There is an economic cost too. High turnover is a significant cost that a company faces if its employees frequently leave due to a toxic work environment.

Being an entrepreneur isn't only about setting up a business and growing it continuously to reach higher milestones. It's also about improving yourself, your skills, and knowledge. Collaboration and delegation are traits that every entrepreneur should master if they are to succeed.

One man alone can't do everything when things have been set in motion, and while you are taking care of the big things that affect a business directly, there are many smaller things that have an impact on a business indirectly.

Internal mayhem can easily be one of those hidden reasons for a company's failure; sometimes, the top leaders are the last to see that. While the top leadership is busy articulating the company's future, its internal friction can lead to inefficiency, low motivation, and decreased productivity.

In the retail sales industry, the employee turnover is usually high; this is often due to the internal inefficiency of the company. There are certainly other reasons—like pay, incentives, atmosphere—but employees who get frustrated with inefficiency may just take a hike.

Customer Experience

Thirty percent of all new businesses fail in the first three years not because they didn't have great products, location, or pricing, but because they had bad customer service.

> 30% OF NEW BUSINESSES FAIL DUE TO BAD CUSTOMER SERVICE.

Put yourself in your customer's shoes and see if you would like the same treatment and experience if you were the customer. If you know of any business that you often go to and love going there because of how they treat you, analyze why, and what you like about them. See if you are offering the same experience to your customers. If not, why?

Apart from these, there can be many other problems that business owners face—from the store atmosphere to experience and staff management. There are all sorts of factors that affect retail sales no matter what kind of business you are running, and to thrive it's important to be aware of them and work on correcting them.

Retail store owners, for instance, are continually faced with the problem of enhancing their customer's store experience and navigation effectiveness. From the moment the customer walks into a store to the time they leave, everything needs to be accounted for. How the sales person greets and assists the customer and whether the products are on display in the most productive way are major concerns for any retail store.

Hiring sales staff that is alike is another problem in retail stores because it limits growth potential. Your customers aren't all alike when it comes to their likes and dislikes, and it's important to have a diversified workforce to cater to all kinds of customers that walk in.

Most patrons don't like being left alone in a store and want the staff at hand to help them navigate or find a particular item. All this relates to how you manage your sales personnel and how warmly they entertain the in-store customer.

Not only should your products be on display at the right places where you know your customers will be able to grab them effortlessly, thus increasing sales, but also, customers should enjoy their shopping experience.

Take for instance Apple's engaging in-store approach, where customers can tinker with new technology and products.

Going to an Apple store is a fun and exhilarating experience for visitors. Aesthetically pleasing designs and interactive displays are the heart of their store. While all stores don't have the resources to go to such lengths to make their in-store experience so memorable, understand that it is important to draw the customer in. If they are enjoying themselves, they likely will spend more money.

There is always something that you can change to enhance your customer's in-store experience significantly. Every store must have a unique look and feel, and that is one thing that most stores lack. Among many other businesses that are exactly like you, that pose competition to you, how do you stand apart from them?

This is another problem in retail sales business that owners need to sort out before they step into reap profits. This issue revolves around branding, but many companies learn that providing greater customer service can also help boost sales.

When you are in a highly competitive market where you must sell the same things as your competitor, what really differentiates you from them is any superior customer service that you can offer. Whether it is home delivery, discounts, after sale product care, free returns or exchanges, online order placement, or faster query response. All of these things go a long way in differentiating one retail unit from another.

Overexpansion

I was guilty of this a few times myself, so I suppose I am the best one to talk about it. When I bought my first fast-food franchise, I was pleasantly surprised to see how simple yet manageable that business was, and how much money I was making.

So in just two years, I grew to five locations, and then overexpansion hit me like a freight train. Over the next two years, for many reasons, (some beyond my control, like the economic meltdown of 2008), I started to suffer financially, mentally, and even physically, as it was hard to manage and supervise all of the locations.

> OVEREXPANSION HIT ME LIKE A FREIGHT TRAIN.

The lesson I learned was while growth is important for business, growing too quickly can also turn into a problem and disrupt the business process. When a company becomes too big without proper procedures in place or by defying the normal growth cycle, it can become difficult to handle.

Problems in logistics, supply, financing and staffing start becoming apparent and the overexpansion, instead of being a step forward, turns into an obstacle in growth. Without a proper strategy and preparation, business growth can stifle the progress of any business, and soon, it may be striving for survival.

It's important for any retail sales business to grow steadily, to have a strategy in place and the right people to execute it. People can make all the difference when it comes to your business making it big or not. Eventually, it's the people who will be doing the work and executing the plan, so the more skilled, diversified, and integrated team that you have running your business, the better results it can help produce.

When hiring management or other staff, it is paramount for a company to hire people who are well aligned with its philosophy and goals. Every company has core values and a centralized philosophy that it stands for. Any misalignment between that and your employees will always cause friction and prevent smooth operations.

Growth is welcome even at a fast pace, but if you don't have the capabilities and resources to handle it, you can find yourself in the midst of mayhem.

Theft, Fraud & Other Crimes

It seems like theft and fraud are almost an inevitable part of the retail business. It is a reality, it is a fact, and it can be anyone, from your vendors to employees, customers, and partners. There is a limited amount of due diligence that a company can perform, but beyond that, avoiding theft and fraud is unavoidable. The best plan of action against theft is to have proper policies and insurance in place to be ready for it if it happens.

You may not be able to stop 100% of the theft or fraud, but as long as you keep it to a minimum, consider yourself lucky. Remember, internal theft and fraud can cost you much more than most external ones. You should be careful and have a formal hiring process in place, which at least allows you to sift candidates based on education, experience, personality, and customer service skills. You can ask for a criminal background check and offer to pay for it.

Apart from the internal and external theft and fraud, there is one more thing we all have to worry about which is a crime against our businesses. Since we are in retail, we deal with cash and often times we are subject to robbery and break-ins. You should have a particular cash handling procedure in place, not more than $100 in any cash register at any given time. The rest has to be dropped into the safe.

Practice safety and coach your employees often, then come and spot check them to see if they are carrying more than $100 in their register at any time. Post a sign on your front door stating that you do not carry more than $100 in your register and that the cashier cannot open the safe. Most large retailers practice these safety procedures and you should too. I will discuss most of these in more detail in a later chapter.

Competition

Last but not least, we need to talk about one of the biggest problems most of us face in our business - competition. It is the unhealthy competition that hurts us the most. When a big name retailer has a location near you, often times they try to undercut you in pricing to steal business from you. Though it is not illegal to do so, in my opinion, it is unethical. Often times they undercut prices where they sell below your cost and essentially force you to do the same.

The best way to battle this war is to win your customers and clients with an outstanding customer service experience. Wow them, bond with them, get to know them. A customer that you know by their first name will come back to your store over and over even if you are little higher on your prices compared to the big name retailers next door.

It is proven, give it a try. No, I am not asking you to increase your prices and charge more. But as long as you are competitive within reason, you can win them over with excellent customer service. People, in general, want that bonding, it is basic human nature.

Learning from Failure

Before we go on, I want to talk about failure. It's important that we take the attitude of: How we can learn from it? It's one of the things I'll be sharing along the way in this book.

Let's go back to my franchise flop. I'll take you through it one painful step at a time. Sounds fun, right? I think it may actually make you feel better about your business's issues, and you can learn from my experience without having to suffer like I did.

That venture went from being a beauty to a beast. I ended up having to declare bankruptcy with my five franchise to-go restaurants. I won't name this particular franchise, but they did specialize in sandwiches and they had national name recognition. In fact, I did so well with this franchise the first few years that I opened three additional locations.

Things were going well for about 6 years until I noticed that sales started to dip. I wondered why, as I had been doing all the same things as before. I had quality products, I had loyal customers, and I had good employees. I had even ordered some specialty drinks and had customers coming in just for those.

BUT SALES GOT WORSE AND WORSE.

Soon I was only doing half the business that I had at my peak. That hurt. Still, I tried to save the business. Lacking funds, I took money out of my own pocket to pay employees.

Then I started to notice some things: There were no ads in the paper or TV any more. That was always something the company had taken care of, as we franchise owners were required to pay monthly fees towards advertising. But the ads had disappeared, and so had my profits.

I also noticed that there were two new sandwich shops that had opened in my area. But then I discovered the really bad news: The parent company was trying to file bankruptcy.

That was when I realized that my business could not be saved. I knew that no amount of money I threw at it was going to make it work. The ship was going down.

So I had to file bankruptcy myself. What did I learn? Well, that was my last dealing with a restaurant franchise. For me, it's not the right fit. I've noticed that new franchises pop up all the time – some last a year, three years, five years, and then they disappear.

I share this story to tell you two things: First, failure is a learning experience. Sounds cheesy I know, but it is the truth.

I learned that I was not interested in another restaurant franchise. I learned that one failed business venture does not mean that you should be done with business altogether. Today I have more than a dozen different businesses. We all can learn from our mistakes. They are some of our most valuable lessons.

Failure is a great teacher.

Second, I want to tell you that throwing more money at a problem is not always the solution. Sometimes there are deeper issues.

So put on your thinking cap and take out your Sherlock Holmes magnifying glass, and let's look at your business. Be ready to learn, even when you identify areas of failure. It's good, because then you can fix the real problem.

Through the course of this entire book, we are going to look at ways to improve your business by identifying weak areas and strengthening them. We will look at three things:

- Where are your pain points or biggest issues?
- What is the cause of these issues?
- How can you fix them?

We will look at some specific areas that are a common problem in small businesses, like securing funding, healthy partnerships, finding/retaining/training employees, selling, marketing, and merchandising. We'll talk about steps you can take to improve in each of these areas.

Truth be told, we can always do better in things like marketing and merchandising, but I hope that as we go through this guide, you will be able to identify your specific pain points and find some real solutions that work for you.

Be honest with yourself and look objectively at your business. What is in the way of growth? Of sales? Is it more than one problem? Has your business changed over time?

Is it hard for you to see where you are doing well and where you could improve? Let's use some tools.

SWOT Analysis

For a fresh perspective, try a SWOT analysis tool: Strengths, Weaknesses, Opportunities, and Threats.

Positive	Negative
Strengths	**Weaknesses**
• Things your company does well • What sets you apart • Best internal resources • Tangible assets, capital, good ideas	• Things your company lacks, could improve • How competitors better • Resource limitations • Unclear unique offerings
Opportunities	**Threats**
• Underserved markets you could supply • What are the growing needs in your area of specialty • Getting media coverage • Drawing in new clients	• Emerging competitors • Changing laws or regulations • Negative press/media coverage • Losing customers

How to use the SWOT Analysis chart: Fill in the bullet points with aspects of your own business. You can do this mentally, or you can take out a sheet of paper, make a simple four-square chart that fills up the page, and begin to fill it in.

For example, in the section under *Strengths,* ask yourself, what are you doing well? Then write down 1-3 things. Then ask yourself, what sets your business apart from the competition? What is special or unique about your business, product, or service? And so on.

Every business has strengths and weaknesses. If you're not sure, ask your employees or your customers. Maybe you carry a great selection of products or have a friendly staff. Or maybe you don't.

Hopefully by the time you complete the entire chart, you will begin to see a realistic picture of what you are doing well, how you could improve, new areas to expand in, or potential threats on the horizon. Then you can use the Table of Contents at the beginning of this book to get helpful input on how to improve in those specific areas.

ID The Real Problem

You need to take a close look at the roots of the issue in your case. Why is this issue a problem?

For example, don't simply say, "Not enough money is coming in." That's too broad of a statement to do you any good. Ask yourself *why*. Try to narrow it down. Look at your profits and losses; look at your pricing; look at your customer base. Take your time and think through the problem: Where is the pain point, specifically?

It won't help much to say simply, "My employees are the problem." Think about the reason, or what exactly they are doing wrong. Are they making mistakes? Then maybe they need more training. Are they unmotivated? Then maybe you need to motivate them with some rewards or a raise or recognition.

Also, it's helpful to get another opinion from someone who is involved in your business whom you trust. You could ask your employees, your partners, or a trusted customer for their thoughts and observations. What am I doing wrong? How do you think I could improve?

If sales are a problem, think that through. Why are you not selling enough? And so on.

Following are a few questions to think about in four different categories. I hope this will get you started in really digging deeper into the cause behind some of your business's specific pain points.

These are think-about-it questions; mull it over and really consider these questions. Then see if you can come up with other, more specific questions suited to your business for each list.

Questions to Consider about Sales

- Have your sales been steadily going up or down? When are your fluctuations?
- Are people interested in your products or services? Why/why not?
- Are you marketing consistently and well using a variety of channels?

- Are you in a good location or a poor one? Is your sign visible? Can people tell what type of business you are from outside?
- Are you connecting with your customers? Do they remember you? Are you fostering loyalty?
- Are your prices high enough so that you make a good return on sales?
- Was there a time when business was better, and why? What changed?
- What is your lowest sales day/month, and how could you draw in more business then?

Questions to Consider about Your Products or Services

- What is my best/worst product? Most popular? Best value? Has that changed?
- What is my greatest strength or weakness as far as services?
- Have my products or services changed over time? Am I improving, growing, and expanding?
- Am I offering more or less in terms of quality? Quantity?

- Do I have a fresh variety of inventory?
- How am I merchandising my products (presenting my products visually)?
- Am I staying on top of trends, new products, what's popular now?
- Have my customers requested anything that I don't carry? Should I order it?
- What is my competition offering that I'm not? What is my competition's best product?
- Do I offer excellent customer service?
- How can I improve my customer's experience & satisfaction?

Questions to Consider about Employees

- What is the best thing about working for me? What do I offer, compared to other employers?
- What is the worst/hardest thing about working for me?
- Do I retain employees or have a high turnover rate?
- How do I reward my best or most faithful employees?
- How could I make them feel valued?

- Are my employees generally happy or do they seem to complain a lot?
- Do my employees seem invested in my business? Why/not?
- How could I give my employees a voice in my business?
- Do my employees deliver excellent customer service? How could they improve?
- How am I trying to motivate them?
- Have I provided adequate training?
- Do I have a system to reward excellent performance?

Questions to Consider about Profits & Losses

- Is my business suffering from theft or shoplifting? If so, where are the vulnerabilities? How is the loss occurring?
- Do I have a system in place to control theft?
- Am I spending too much on my products?
- Am I selling my product or service for the right price?
- Am I being undercut by my competitors; if so, how are they able to sell for less?

If you're still not sure what your problem areas are, or the roots of those issues, don't worry. We're going to learn about common reasons why small businesses fail and how to solve them.

One of the biggest ones is in the next chapter: financial challenges. This is a common problem whether you're just starting out or you have hit a wall in your established business.

Chapter 2 – Financial Challenges

Financial challenges in business—we all deal with them. Whether you are starting a brand-new business or hitting a wall in your current business, the most important need of the small business owner is usually money.

In this section, I want to talk about some ways to secure funding, types of funding, and finding new partnerships and investors.

Funding Sources

If you're just starting out, there are few ways to go about finding the required funds. You can also use this list if you have hit a financial snag in your business and you're trying to think of ways to inject a fresh boost of funds into your business in order to expand or take it to the next level.

1. **Your own savings/401K**

If you truly believe that your business will be profitable, or if your need is short-term—you can dip into your own savings or your 401K.

The plus side is that this is ready money. You have it already; it's easy to get to. The downside, obviously, is that you are taking a great financial risk by using your own savings if you have no backup plan for yourself or the business.

2. **Home equity line of credit**

This is a secured loan that is backed by using your equity in your home as collateral. This is actually how I started my business.

You can establish it ahead of time and use it only when/if/how you need it. Home equity loans have very similar pros/cons to the first option, as you are risking the collateral in your home.

3. Family funding

Basically, this is where your parents, siblings, or other family members help you with a personal loan. Even though they are family, please do put the terms in writing regarding how much they are lending you and how long you have to pay it back.

4. Create partnership with people who have money to invest in your business.

If you don't want to simply take your family member's money, you could offer to make them a partner in your business. There are several types of partnerships, as we will discuss later in this chapter.

You certainly want to put into writing what the partnership entails, as not all partners have the same power in business decisions, etc. You will create an operating agreement which all the partners read and sign. This will protect all involved and make the terms crystal clear.

5. Crowdfunding

This is where you publicly ask people to invest in your business or product or idea in order to generate income. There are a growing number of platforms to use, including Kickstarter, GoFundMe, Crowdfunder, LendingClub, Patreon. If you choose to, you can offer your supporters some kind of incentive (free products or specialty items), or you can update them on your progress and success. More on this later.

6. Applying for a small business loan at your local bank

This option takes a little more time but is perhaps the best way to go if you need a large amount of money. You will still need some form of collateral as well as a solid business plan.

Because this option can be complex and is very important, we will look at coming up with a business plan and applying for a bank loan in the next chapters.

Sit down, take out a piece of paper, and brainstorm through each of these options. Considering your situation, need, and business—try to analyze each and every option and then see which one seems more doable for you.

You can even mix and match these sources. For example, if you need $100,000 to open your bakery business but you only have $50,000, one idea is to ask one or two like-minded friends or family to come in as a 50% partner, where you hold 50% of the business, and the other two get 25% each.

In this next section, we will talk about investors, partners, and crowdfunding. I'll give you some details options and tips that I've picked up from my own life experiences and that of other successful business owners.

INVESTORS AND PARTNERS

As long as you are honest, dependable, and hardworking, there are people out there willing to invest with you. Those who do have money but don't have the resources or time to start or run a business. Partnering with you in your business will be an alliance that is profitable for both of you.

When you bring in an outside person to join you in funding or running your business, there are two types: **active** and **passive**. I will call the passive people **investors**, as they are really just supplying funding and will not have an active role in your business. The active investors I will call **partners**, because they are partnering with you in the business, on a variety of levels, depending on your preference.

Investors

After personal assets, an **Angel Investor** is the most common source of funds in the U.S. This type of investor is also called a **silent partner**.

An Angel Investor is a private investor who supports a business financially—typically one who invests private capital in a small or newly established enterprise. Even though they are a silent partner, Angel Investors will want to see a business plan, objectives, goals, strategy, and projections before meeting with you. (Read the chapter on creating a solid business plan.)

A silent partner is essentially saying, I will put my credit or my cash on the line for your business. They will have liquid assets (cash), and will have good credit to help you get that loan very easily. Or they may pay the whole startup cost as a loan, with an agreement about how you will pay it back—such as paying them the mortgage payment of the building plus some percentage of the profits every month.

Even though they are a silent partner, they will more than likely want a stake in your restaurant or business in exchange for their investment, such as a percentage of the profits.

If you don't know anyone with investment capital, you can find them in investment clubs and venture capitalist groups online or locally. Their trade group is called the Angel Capital Association. Their website **angelcapitalassociation.org** even lists regional angel groups by location in the US or other parts of the world. Their website also has a section for entrepreneurs with resources and links – definitely worth a read.

Partners

You also have the option of funding via a **partnership**. A partner is another person who contracts with you to help grow your business.

For all partnerships, you must share a common goal, have a commitment to the business, similar expectations and ethics, and mutual trust. I talk more in depth about 5 Keys to a Successful Partnership later on. First, let's look at three types of partnerships:

Three Types of Partnerships

Working Partner

The term 'working partner' may sound confusing. It simply means somebody who is willing to do some work in the business as opposed to a silent or no active partner. Perhaps you are looking to invest in a similar business, looking for a partner willing to work and partner with you to make your joint business profitable. Perhaps one person is short on funds but they are looking to take on the work in order to make up for the lack of capital.

Let's say you found a business that costs $100,000, and you found a partner who can invest $20,000 but is also willing to work as part of their contribution (or vice versa). That may work for you. Let me say this: A partner must invest *something*. If you get a partner who does not invest a dime and they don't have any skin in the game, they may not value the business as highly as you would because only your money is invested in that business.

Whatever money they have, take that into the business. Your terms may be something like this: Even though they only invested $20K, you will still give them 50% partnership as long as they pay you back the difference from profit every month. In this case it would be $30,000 that they would have to pay you back before they can take any profit home. I have done this system before, and it works wonderfully

Now, it doesn't have to be a 50/50 partnership; it can be 20/80 or whatever way you want to structure it – as long as you have a clear understanding with that person and a written, signed **operating agreement**.

How would you figure out your terms? You could do some future projected Profit and Losses, figure that the business should generate 4-6% profit a month, and then they will pay you a certain amount or percentage every month out of their share of profit so that their loan can be paid off in some predetermined time (or vice versa, in case you are the one doing the work and your partner is the one putting up the majority of the funds). This takes into account the expected profitability of that business and makes sure there is a realistic goal of how to pay off the loan/investment of the funding partner.

Equal Partners

Meaning you are equal, you're both sharing responsibilities in your partnership. Let's say you own and operate a business. You want to invest in a second business, but you have limited time, funds, and resources. You find a similar minded person who has another store they operate themselves. They too have limited funds and time available. You can partner with that individual. You decide to create a partnership where we are equal in every sense, equal responsibility and equal money invested.

Operating a business takes a lot of time and varied responsibilities. In an equal partnership, you still need to sit down and draw up the specifics. Put in writing (with an operating agreement) who has what responsibility.

Things to clarify: Who will hire employees, make the schedule, and supervise them? Who will deal with vendors and order supplies? Who will do the bookkeeping and payroll? Merchandising, marketing?

What would this look like? If you have a strength with employees and merchandising, you take those responsibilities. But keep in mind there cannot be two bosses. You don't want a two-headed monster. So if you're handling the employees, make sure you call a meeting of employees and let them know how the chain of command works. Don't have two/multiple bosses, as some employees may try to take advantage of that: "He told me to do this," overriding what you told them to do. It's important to establish that chain of command.

If one of my partners is responsible for handling employees and I have other duties, I always let employees know that they have to talk to their boss, not me, if they need a day off or a raise. Let's say I'm there doing merchandising or vendor control; even though I'm a partner, I still do not get involved in that part of the business. If you make that clear, employees will respect that, and this will eliminate silly mistakes and confusion.

If you're responsible for handling vendors and doing orders, then as long as you do your job properly and you let your partner do the other half, things should go smoothly. You each have to feed from each other's strengths and not weaknesses. You have to support each other.

If a partner goes out of town, then make sure she/he has told the employees that you will be acting as full manager, in charge. Then you can authorize a day off or a schedule change because they all know that you are in charge for the time being.

But never override your partner's decisions in his/her arena of responsibility. In turn, you would not expect them to override your responsibilities or duties. If you don't keep to the agreed roles, it creates confusion and hurts your relationship with vendors and employees, as well as the mutual trust between partners.

Success Tips:

Lay it all out in writing, and it should be fine. This is called an operating agreement and needs to be signed by all partners.

There may be times when one of you needs a few days off, and you need to hand over your job duties to the other. That's why it's so important to have an understanding.

A business partnership is unique relationship. There is a type of bonding, a professional friendship, and mutual respect. In a sense, you have a sort of dependency and trust in your partner. This is a good thing.

Still, keep a clear boundary between business and friendship. You are not best buddies with your partner; you are colleagues. Try to keep out of each other's personal life, since that can create friction. Keep a healthy boundary so that you can still have a good understanding, respect, and trust.

Multiple Partners With One Key Operating Person

This is a partnership in which 3 or 4 similar minded people want to invest in your business, but they don't want to get into day-to-day operations. Everyone's goal is to increase their income.

First, find a capable, hardworking, honest person who is looking to get into business but does not have the funds (this can be you, if you have low resources, or it can be another person if you do have some funds to invest). Let that person run the store or the daily operations. That person becomes the chief/key operating person. It is essentially a working partnership with multiple partners who are not involved in the details on a daily basis.

As I say often, make sure you have everything in writing in an operating agreement that spells out how everything will be done from A to Z: how to handle employees, ordering, budget, operating expenses, and expected profitability.

This is very important for this type of partnership: Make sure you have a clear picture of how the P&L (profit and loss) should look for the next year or two. How it's doing now and how it will look in future. I'll explain why this is so important in a moment.

You can calculate your P&L projection based on current sales. If you don't make any major changes to that business, and it doesn't suddenly decrease when the key operating person takes over—then you can reasonably project that it will make roughly the same amount in profit.

Or if you do improvements (ads, marketing, products, location upgrades, special offers, etc.), then you can predict that sales will go up by maybe 2 or 3% in your P&L forecast. You can even do two sets of forecasts: If the sales remain the same, then the expected annual amount of profit should be x. If the sales increase due to improvements, then the annual sales could reach y.

Why is it so important to project sales with multiple partners? Because you want to ensure that they are in it for the long term, that everyone has realistic expectations, and that one of the partners will not try to cut and run before a reasonable amount of time has been given to let the business succeed. Everyone needs to be all in for a reasonable amount of time. It's only fair, and it's good business.

In my opinion, I think it's reasonable to ask partners to stay with the business agreement for 1-3 years at least. I always hope my sales will be profitable in the first few months, and then everyone will want to stay involved for a longer period instead of wanting to take their profits and run.

To reiterate some important steps to ensuring a healthy partnership, here are my 5 Keys to a Successful Partnership.

5 Keys to Successful Partnerships

1. All partners must have some potential **stake** in the business. Every partner should have some skin in the game, some type of invested interest in game. If not, they will not value the business or do their best.

2. All partners must be working toward a **common goal.** Every partner's goal should be the same, to make the business a success.

3. All partners should have **similar ethics** or system of beliefs. If one partner is not as ethical, then you could have a serious potential problem. If one wants to take shortcuts, then in your absence things can go wrong if they are not done properly. Everybody's ethics have to be high, and the shared belief system has to be there. Our main goal is to make the business a success, the right way.

4. All partners must agree to work together over a **reasonable period of time**. This should be in writing in the operating agreement with their

signature. All partners should understand that it may take 4 months to a year to see much profit. Some businesses need to be built up for several years to see real profitability. Each partner needs to understand the required time it takes to build the business up and the length of time it may take for them to see a return on their investment.

You do not want a partner showing up after a month or two saying, "I want my profit now." I have seen this, and it's not a good situation. This is where a potential partnership breakdown can start. It is too difficult to tell in the midst of the year what the profits really are. At the end of the year, the accountant will do a form called a K-1 which reports each partner's share of the profits.

5. Each partner should be willing to **share their expertise** to help the business succeed. Understanding the value of what each partner can contribute is key. Let's say one partner is good with accounting, merchandising, and customer service. They need to bring their best

abilities or knowledge forward to make the business successful.

Even if you have a key operating person and silent partners, those silent partners may have valuable insight to share. Why not ask them to step in or speak up for a time to help the business grow and make more money. They may say, "I didn't invest to work," but it does not hurt to ask them help the business to thrive at the startup, just temporarily. They can contribute their expertise and improve the business they have already invested in.

Without a strong partnership, there is little chance for success. As the saying goes: United we stand; divided we fall. It means you gain from each other's strengths to overcome weaknesses and ensure a strong business and good profit overall.

CROWDFUNDING

Crowdfunding is when you raise money to finance a new business venture through small contributions from a large number of people, usually through the internet.

> IN 2015, OVER $34 BILLION USD WAS RAISED WORLDWIDE BY CROWDFUNDING.

As we go more in depth about crowdfunding, I'd like to talk about two different approaches: First, the most common way; second, a consortium or partnership style that might be more ideal for a small business owner like yourself. Then we will look at some success tips for how to use crowdfunding for your small business.

Two Approaches to Crowdfunding

The normal method for crowdfunding is that you create a page through an online platform or website (like GoFundMe or Kickstarter, etc.) get the word out through social media, and allow anyone who sees the page or is interested to contribute to your project.

If you are unfamiliar with the concept of crowdfunding or how it works, I encourage you to take a look at kickstarter.com to see how it's done.

First, people come to the site and post their project—this could be something in the arts, film, food, music, publishing, all different sorts of things. They give the details of their specific project along with a budget (called a goal) of a fixed dollar amount. They usually say why they are qualified, what experience or skills they have, and share their story and goals.

For example, they may say, *I will create a book about Asian cooking for keto, since I have been on the keto diet for 4 years and I am a chef trained in Asian-style cooking.* They share their motivation: *I have always dreamed of helping others who enjoy Asian food to find healthy alternatives that provide more protein and less carbs.* There should also be some photographs or images—maybe of the main person who started the project or a book cover, etc.

They will also give some sort of incentive. For example, the first 100 people who donate $100 will get a signed copy of their book. Or, those who donate $50 or more will get a copy of the book without a signature. Or, anyone who donates $10 or more will get an eBook. Usually in the incentives, the more someone pays, the more they get. Sometimes they will even mention the people in the book who helped fund the project.

That is the first, most common way that crowdfunding works. For a small business, you would not want to try to raise all of your startup capital or have an ongoing fundraiser with no end in sight; it likely would not work. The platform isn't really designed for that. People like feasible amounts with clear goals/projects. So you could do a kickstarter campaign to refurbish your commercial kitchen, and offer your backers free pies or even an entire Thanksgiving dinner for pledging certain amounts.

A second type of crowdfunding—an alliance or consortium style—may be more appropriate for you or your business, depending on how much you need to raise, your network of contacts, and your business niche.

To form an alliance type of crowdfunding for your small business, you can make your crowdfunding more personal and focused than the usual method.

For example: Make a list of 10-20 people that you know. Ask each of them for an investment of

$10,000 for a 7% stake in your company. If 10 of them agree, you will have $100,000, and you only gave out 70% of your business. The remaining 30% is still yours for FREE.

This is sort of a hybrid between normal crowdfunding and having multiple business partners. But it's much simpler than typical partnerships. These people are simply funding your business; there is no need for P&L reports or shared responsibilities or shared risk or their name on the business loans, etc.

Success Tips for Crowdfunding

1. **Do your research.** Look around at websites like Kickstarter, GoFundMe, Indiegogo, Wefunder, or Fundable. Look for successful projects in your sphere. See what their specific projects/goals are, how they present their project, what incentives they use. Get your creative, entrepreneurial wheels turning and see what's actually working for small businesses like yours.

2. **Have a strong business plan or idea.** You need something specific and attainable that people will want to get behind. Instead of saying you want to open your own business because it's been a dream of yours (which is me-focused)—rather, talk about the need for a coffee shop that offers alternative types of coffees, and how your store will benefit consumers and be good for the environment (which is consumer-focused). Why would someone get behind your project? Appeal to their values or likes.

3. **Compare different platforms & their terms.** They each have a bit of a different approach and market. They have different billing policies, may have age requirements, and may prohibit certain types of industries or products. Make sure it's right for you.

4. **Be ready to market your project.** You need a website, something where people can go to learn more about you, your product, or your business. Market it well. You will need to spread the word through all of the social media

platforms you can. Send out emails if you have a D-list. Get your friends or customers to spread the word. Some businesses who have a brick-and-mortar store will put a sign in their business about their Kickstarter campaign to add more organic choices to the menu, etc.

5. **Line up investors in advance.** Most people will only back something if they can see that other people have already backed it. Friends and family work fine for a few initial investors, and they will add credibility and boost confidence of other backers.

6. **Choose the right type of campaign:** Donation campaigns are when people give you money with no promise of anything in return. Debt campaigns are like a loan, in which you agree to pay back the money given with interest. Rewards usually offer backers an incentive based on how much they donate (as mentioned previously with the signed book example). Equity gives investors a percentage of ownership in your business in return for their funds. Spell this out clearly.

So, as you can see, you have a lot of options for finding financing. Remember when there is a strong will power to achieve something, there is always a way to get there.

> BE CREATIVE AND CONSIDER ALL OF YOUR CHOICES. WHAT WORKS BEST FOR YOU?

Applying for a loan at the bank is the hardest of all the methods above. That's why I will go into detail in the next chapters about what you will need to apply for a bank loan and how to create a strong business plan to ensure success.

CHAPTER 3 – GETTING A BANK LOAN

Maybe financing is an issue for you. If you've never gotten a small business loan from the bank, let me walk you through it. One thing that you will need to present to the bank is a well-thought-out, professional business plan. See the next chapter for specifics on what should be in your business plan.

In this chapter, we'll look at: Choosing the right bank for your loan, three different types of financial needs and financing, options for financing, and how much you really need.

Choosing the Right Bank

In the event that you have no other option but to apply for a loan, you must do some research first.

First come up with a list of banks you want to apply to. It is not a good idea to apply at multiple banks at once; instead, come up with a list of four banks. Visit of them and talk in depth with their business loan department and find out if that bank offers loans for your type of projects. For example, there are banks that do not offer loans for restaurants. So find out what your options are.

In my experience, I have noticed typically smaller local banks are more inclined to offer loans to local family-owned bakeries, restaurants, coffee shops, and other similar businesses than some of the bigger banks are. But that may not be true for every part of the country, so it is best to talk to at least 3-4 banks and try to get a feel for whether they are really into your sort of business financing or not—before you submit your application.

Sometimes your local business brokers or commercial real estate agents can guide you to the right bank as they often deal with similar situations and knows which banks are more favorable to these sort of loans. You can also contact your bank that you deal with every day and ask for their advice.

Now once you have narrowed it down to two banks, visit them, have a meeting with their loan officer and see what their requirements are. Just remember that, even though every bank will have similar requirements, they can still vary widely based on many factors: how much down payment they require, how much collateral they will need from you, whether they offer SBA-assisted loans or not. Your goal would be to deal with a bank that offers SBA loans (SBA stands for Small Business Administration).

Some of the larger banks that deal with SBA loans are Wells Fargo, Chase Bank, U.S. Bank, Bank of America, and T.D. Bank. Though sometimes it's best to choose the bank you already have a relationship with when applying for a loan. Just know all of your options.

Different Types of Loans

You have several options when it comes to the types of loans. Let me walk you through two of the most common.

What is an SBA Loan?

In an SBA loan, the federal government guarantees part of your loan to the bank. Usually, the SBA guarantees 50-80% of your loan to the bank, so banks are somewhat more lenient in approving the loan as they are not taking on the risk for the total amount. The downside to SBA loans is that you have a monumental amount of paperwork.

SBA loan requirements can be broad and extensive, so be prepared to hunt down records and fill out many forms.

Another drawback to an SBA loan is that it can take 4-6 months to get approval as they run slower than most banks. In their defense, they do have a lot of applicants and have to go through all of them. It is always 'first come, first served', so be patient.

Conventional Business Loan

But if you have a larger down payment (30% or higher) or some good collateral to offer, then you can opt out of going with an SBA loan and instead get a conventional business loan. Most banks will approve this, provided you have all your ducks in a row: Your credit is in excellent shape, your tax returns show good income for previous years, you have a good business plan, and so on.

What are your options for getting financing to open and run your small business? How much financing do you need?

THREE TYPES OF CAPITAL

Financing is not just a one-time deal. There are three steps of financing that you need.

1. Seed Capital

This is money for start-up, preparing your restaurant for opening followed by operating costs for a period of time before profits are made.

2. Growth Capital

Funds to grow your business once you have proven it is a feasible concept and you are up and running.

3. Harvest Cash

This is cash needed for when a partner, investor, or an owner wants their money out of the restaurant.

You have all this information built into your business plan. You need to have money for any of the above events six to nine months before it's needed.

Your **seed capital** or start-up is what you need to open. What are you going to put in your business plan? $80,000, $550,000, a million? Once you have determined what you need, don't undersell yourself. You may think asking for less will make it easier to get approved. Don't risk it.

Also, your banker or investor will need to see the use of these funds outlined in your business plan. For instance, do you need it all at once? Can a percentage be available but not drawn on until another stage?

For instance, your **growth capital** stage. These funds will be needed when you require a cash injection to continue growth to the point of stable profit-making.

You will also need a line of credit. Here's how that works. You project $80,000 in sales per month and want to have a two-month safety net of $160,000 cash. This is funding you will need to get from your banker as a line of credit.

> A LINE OF CREDIT SERVES AS A
> SAFETY NET FOR START-UPS.

LOAN PACKAGE & DOCUMENTATION

When you talk to any banks, they will hand you something called a loan package. Most times the package will have a checklist of documents that they want you to furnish to them along with a loan application and some other waiver forms, depending on your bank.

One thing to keep in mind: all banks and commercial lenders do have to follow certain guidelines that are set by federal and state banking authorities. Also, every bank will look at something called the LTV (Loan to Value) ratio of the property or business you are looking to buy. LTV is essentially where banks look at the actual value of the business you are looking to buy and how much of that value they can loan you.

But in any case, let's look at the list of documents you will need to get ready to submit to your bank. Some of these items I will mention here may not be on your bank's checklist but do gather them anyway as it will make you look more professional and business-like.

Items You Will Need from the Seller:
- Last two years of P&L
- Last three years Tax Returns of the business
- A balance sheet
- Any and all health and equipment inspection reports and repair estimates

What You Need to Gather:

1. You need to get copies of at least last 3 years of tax returns. Make sure the copies are signed.

2. Your resume (they may not even ask you for it, but remember the person that may approve your loan may never meet you but this way at least he or she gets to see who you are and how qualified you are. It always helps)

3. Copy of your Corp. Articles, (yes, you have to get this done before you even apply for your loan.)

4. Personal financial statement for all Corp. Officers or members. Make sure to sign it. If you are married and file joint tax returns, then your wife needs to have one prepared for her as well. Or you can make a joint personal financial statement for both of you and make sure you both sign that document.

5. Copy of the commercial appraisal (if applicable)

6. Copy of signed purchase agreement and Letter of Intent (if buying an existing business)

7. Copy of your EIN (Employer's Identification Number) issued by the IRS

8. Copy of all member/partner's Driver's licenses and social security cards

9. A well-thought-out and expertly written Business Plan (see the chapter on "A Solid Business Plan" for how to do this step by step.)

10. Last but not least, the loan application all filled out (use a computer and printer if possible; if not, write very clearly, so it is easy to read)

11. A cover letter addressed to the loan officer describing what is in the package and thanking them for reviewing your loan application (see an example in the "Business Plan" chapter)

CHAPTER 4 – LEGAL MATTERS

In this section, we'll talk about the importance of bookkeeping and software options, small business taxes and deductions, and choosing the right structure or type for your business. *Note:* I am not a lawyer or a CPA, so please hire a professional for legal and accounting advice. I am sharing from my personal experience only.

What does your bookkeeping look like? Please tell me you aren't just skating by with a simple check register and legal pad. If you are, it's time to start keeping detailed and accurate records. In fact, it's imperative to your success and survival as a small business in the long term.

I cannot stress enough how important it is to keep good, clear, accurate records of *everything* related to your business. You need a system to keep track of your **expenses** (everything from vendor prices and purchases, equipment costs, and your mortgage, electric bill, etc.) as well as your **payroll** (keeping employee information in a secure location) and your **revenues** (all profits and money coming in).

There are many reasons for the need for accuracy and monthly bookkeeping that you may not have considered. For one, you could be audited. Now, if you make less than $100,000 a year in gross receipts, the likelihood of you being audited is very low, statistically. If you make more than $200,000, the likelihood goes up (according to the IRS 2018

Data Book). Being prepared will give you peace of mind and protect your assets. If you expect to be audited and plan for that, then you won't be taken off guard.

For another reason, you will need to show records to your financial partners and lending institutions.

If you ever need to produce records for legal reasons, then you have them at hand. And of course, if you should ever want to sell your business, your future buyer will want to see detailed records of the business's profits and losses.

Accurate and thorough records don't have to be complicated. But they need to be done right. How do you keep tabs of your monthly profits and losses? You need digital records, and you need to periodically back them up on a thumb drive. Depending on how complex your business is, you may only need a simple spreadsheet. I used Excel to create my monthly P&L statements for years:

<u>Jackie's Wash & Fold Laundromat</u>
Profit and Loss Statement
December, 2016

Store Revenue:	Sales $	
Washer	6,750.00	
Dryer	4,050.00	
Wash & Fold	5,250.00	
Video Game Machine	650.00	
Deli Food Sales	2,500.00	
Vending Sales	1,250.00	
Cost of Goods Sold	750.00	
Gross Profit:		19,700.00
Store Expenses:		
Payroll	3,950.00	
Utility	4,500.00	
Rent	2,750.00	
Insurance	650.00	
C.C. Charge	127.00	
Maintenance	780.00	
License & Mics	150.00	
Security	100.00	
Misc.	50.00	
Total Expense		13,057.00
Net Profit:		6,643.00

ACCOUNTING SOFTWARE

The most common software used for accounting is QuickBooks. It used to be a lot more complicated, but it has gotten easier to use over time. If you're an independent contractor or sole proprietor who only needs to manage invoices, then FreshBooks may work better for you. But if you have products and employees, I recommend QuickBooks.

If you don't like QuickBooks, two others I have heard good things about are NetSuite and ZarMoney.

That said, I do have an accountant who keeps the books for all of my LLCs. It's just easier. If you don't need one full time, you can hire an accountant or CPA on an hourly basis; make sure they are certified for tax filings.

A CPA or small business accountant who knows the ins and outs of small businesses and deductions is worth their weight in gold. Not only can they keep your records straight, but they can advise you on audit triggers that could flag an IRS audit.

Make sure you are categorizing your expenses. Otherwise, your accountant or CPA will have a real mess on their hands. Keep track of all of the ins and outs, all of the transactions. QuickBooks even has a daily sales feature, so be sure to use it.

Keeping Good Records

Make sure you have a separate business banking account so that personal and business finances stay separated.

What do you spend money on for your business? Write it all down. Keep the receipts. Paper cups, business lunches, fuel, signage, equipment. It all needs to be kept track of. If you don't want to be neck-deep in paper receipts, then you can use an online accounting software to scan and keep track of your receipts.

How to organize your receipts? Two apps that are designed for scanning and saving receipts are Receipt Bank and Shoeboxed. You can even mail in paper receipts to Shoeboxed and have them scanned for you.

Whatever you do, do not simply throw those receipts away. If you do take someone out to lunch for business, it helps to keep track of who that client was and that it was a business meeting, etc.

Good records will help show that you are honest. Make sure they are easy to find and understand. Bad records or saying "I don't know" too often in an audit will not look good for you.

Above all else, be organized. Have an organized system to track your income, expenses, payroll, and other business transactions. If an auditor asked for an explanation of $2,700 in meals and entertainment, could you provide proof that it was a business expense? Thinking ahead and staying organized is your best line of defense.

Small Business Taxes

As I said, I am not a legal expert on small business taxes, so I will not give you much specific advice about how to do your taxes here. What I will talk about are some general guidelines about exemptions and deductions for a small business.

I highly recommend that you visit the sba.gov website to learn more about business taxes, filing, forms, and deductions. And, of course, hire a qualified professional to do your taxes—especially if you are not a simple sole proprietor. But even then, if your business structure is complex, you may want to hire a professional.

Tax Deductions: What Can I Write Off?

You may not have considered this, but the biggest benefit of owning your own business is that you can write off your business expenses for tax deductions.

Things that are considered business expenses:

- Phone bill (the percentage used for the business)
- Internet cost (percentage used for business)
- Travel expenses for business reasons
- Your car expenses (all or part) if used for business deliveries or transporting goods or supplies, etc.
- Home office expenses, like a computer, desk, or chair
- Business meals
- Business insurance
- Home repairs, rent, utilities (depending on the square footage you use for the business)

Keep all of your receipts and documentation handy, for your own records and any audits. You would be surprised how quickly this all adds up!

The IRS defines **business expenses** as "the cost of carrying on a trade or business. These expenses are usually deductible if the business operates to make a profit."

What can I deduct?

To be deductible, a business expense must be "both ordinary and necessary," according to the IRS. They define an ordinary expense as one that is "common and accepted in your trade or business." Also, they define a necessary expense as one that is "helpful and appropriate for your trade or business. An expense does not have to be indispensable to be considered necessary."

That said, they recommend that you separate such business expenses from the following expenses:

- Expenses used to figure the cost of goods sold,
- Capital Expenses

- Personal Expenses

Cost of Goods Sold

How do you calculate the cost of goods sold?

If your small business produces products or purchases them for resale, you should value your inventory at the beginning and end of each tax year to determine your cost of goods sold (unless you are a small business taxpayer).

Some of your expenses may be included in determining the cost of the goods you sell. The IRS states, "The cost of goods sold is deducted from your gross receipts to figure your gross profit for the year. If you include an expense in the cost of goods sold, you cannot deduct it again as a business expense"

- These expenses below are part of determining the cost of goods sold (per irs.gov).
- The cost of products or raw materials, including freight
- Storage

- Direct labor costs (including contributions to pensions or annuity plans) for workers who produce the products
- Factory overhead

If you are a small business taxpayer who has average annual gross receipts of $25 million or less for the three previous tax years and is not a tax shelter, a different set of rules may apply to you for what you can deduct from your taxes. To learn more about being a small business taxpayer, I recommend you read IRS Publication 224 updated in 2020, called "Tax Guide for Small Businesses."

Capital Expenses

Not all business purchases can be deducted, especially if they are assets. For example, the cost of purchasing a business vehicle cannot be deducted from your gross income for that year because it becomes part of your assets. This means you list it as a capital expense, something that will add value to your business over time. You likely may be able to deduct it over time. Talk to your tax professional about specific large purchases like major equipment, buildings, vehicles, etc.

According to the IRS: Capital expenses are considered assets in your business. In general, there are three types of costs you capitalize.

- Business start-up costs (See the note below)
- Business assets
- Improvements

Other Types of Business Expenses*

Employees' Pay - You can generally deduct the pay you give your employees for the services they perform for your business.

Retirement Plans - Retirement plans are savings plans that offer you tax advantages to set aside money for your own, and your employees' retirement.

Rent Expense - Rent is any amount you pay for the use of property you do not own. In general, you can deduct rent as an expense only if the rent is for property you use in your trade or business. If you have or will receive equity in or title to the property, the rent is not deductible.

Interest - Business interest expense is an amount charged for the use of money you borrowed for business activities.

Taxes - You can deduct various federal, state, local, and foreign taxes directly attributable to your trade or business as business expenses.

Insurance - Generally, you can deduct the ordinary and necessary cost of insurance as a business expense, if it is for your trade, business, or profession.*

Note: This list is not all inclusive; for more information, refer to IRS Publication 535, "Business Expenses." *Source: irs.gov.*

BUSINESS STRUCTURES

What type of business do you have? Is it a sole proprietorship? Is it time to become an LLC?

Types of Businesses

There are several different types of businesses ranging from sole proprietorship, partnerships, LLCs, and various types of corporations. Let's take a look at three common types of small businesses. Here are some differences, with pros and cons for each.

Sole Proprietorship	Partnership	LLC
• Owned and operated by one person. • **Advantages:** Easy to start, owner makes all decisions, keeps all profits, is his/her own boss. • **Disadvantages:** Owner liable for all debts and assets, must work long hours. Difficult to raise capital to start. All risk falls on owner.	• Owned and operated by 2+ people. Each contributes money, property, labor or skill; shares profits &losses. • **Advantages:** Easy to start, more ways to raise capital, shared skills and decisions. • **Disadvantages:** Each partner is liable for debts, can make decisions, share profits. Conflict possible.	• A hybrid business entity that combines aspects of a coproration and partnership. • **Advantages:** Offers limited liability protection, tax deductions and flexibility. • **Disadvantages:** Profits may be subject to self-employment taxes.

The most common small business type is the sole-proprietorship, mostly because it's the simplest to register if you're a new business owner. It makes sense, too – you're the owner, after all, so why wouldn't you register as such? When you register your business as a sole-proprietorship, you're telling the government that you are the only business owner, no one else owns a single piece of your business, and it's all your responsibility.

The biggest bonus for sole-proprietorship is that you don't have to file separate business taxes – everything gets rolled into your own personal taxes, and it does save time. In my opinion, it's the best option if you are not earning much income yet.

Another option is to register your business as a partnership if someone else is sharing the cost and responsibility. A more common option that will give you some professional protection and tax breaks is creating an LLC.

An LLC, or Limited Liability Company, gives you an extra layer of protection. If something happens to the business, if you go under, if you're sued, etc., *you* as an individual will not be held responsible. Instead, the *company* itself is held responsible. If you go bankrupt and have to liquidate, or the LLC owes money, they can only go after the shared property and property *of the business*. They cannot pursue you personally.

Yes, when put like that, an LLC makes *so much* more sense. I highly, highly encourage you to create an LLC for your business. Is it a little more work? Yes, absolutely. And I hope that you will never *need* that extra insurance that an LLC provides. But it's a safety net that every new business should have.

Assuming you want to register as an LLC, I'll quickly take you through the basic steps.

Registering an LLC

First, you're going to need to go on your state's Secretary of State Website and get the LLC Articles of Organization form. For most states, this can be accessed online, but (rarely) you may need to pick up the form in person. Most places will, at the very least, mail it to you.

Fill out the Articles of Organization form, and look into what other requirements your state has. Some states require you to publish something called a notice of intention to form your LLC in your local newspaper. This is quite outdated and is being heavily phased out, but some places will not consider your LLC legal if you don't. *If you don't have to* by law, don't bother wasting the money.

The third and final step is to submit your completed form, along with a filing fee, to the Secretary of State. Each state has a different filing fee – some are just $50, while others are several hundred. Some states will also require you to pay a corporate tax upfront at the time of filing, so be sure to include that as well if you need to.

Also, rarely, some states require an LLC annual report fee. Make sure to find out what your state requires ahead of time, so you're not surprised.

BUSINESS INSURANCE OPTIONS

There are a few types of insurance we need to address. They are all important, and you should put a lot of consideration into them before moving forward. As a professional business, insurance is essential to protecting you, your company, and your customers.

I have heard from new small business owners that they planned to skip small business insurance because they didn't feel it was that important.

They are wrong. Business insurance is vital because it protects you and your company from a variety of issues – some obvious, some not so obvious. Many of which could be very serious.

Business insurance is vital.

A good business insurance won't just cover you when it comes to medical expenses, bodily harm, or property damage, but it will also help handle slander accusations, defend you against lawsuits, protect you from libel, and handle any settlements or judgments associated with these things.

Insurance covers a lot more than just accidents at work, and it's worth every penny when something happens. Every single successful business has some sort of insurance.

Product liability insurance protects you against financial loss from a defective product that causes harm. If you purchase a bad batch of something and it hurts someone, essentially, product liability insurance covers you. It's vital that you follow the proper manufacturing process, however, or your insurance will never pay out your claim.

Commercial property insurance covers any loss or damage to the company's property. This can include raw materials, the finished product, equipment, the workshop building itself, even a craft show display. Anything the company owns, generally speaking, commercial property insurance can cover.

Finally, there is one more: the **home-based business owner's insurance**. This provides an extra layer of protection for home-based businesses on top of personal home insurance. Generally, this covers a small amount of equipment, plus some limited liability in case someone else gets hurt.

I encourage you to read your home insurance policy thoroughly before you sign up for this. Some home insurance policies are completely voided when you work out of your home on a personal business, while others may just raise the premium.

SOME HOME INSURANCE POLICIES
ARE VOIDED WHEN YOU WORK OUT OF
YOUR HOME.

Insurance can be overwhelming, so I encourage you to take it slow. Consult multiple companies, and compare premiums. Ask questions – what is covered? Is everything in the business covered, or just a few things? How much coverage do you actually need?

Find out if there is a revenue cap. Sometimes when insurance companies are catering to small businesses, they have a revenue cap on their plans – this is so that larger businesses don't take advantage of the policies. Be sure the revenue cap is well within your projections.

You will never regret protecting yourself, your customers, and your business.

Chapter 5 – A Solid Business Plan

If I were a bank, the first thing I would expect to see is a solid business plan. Do you have a business plan? What is it? What is it for?

The best way I can describe a business plan is that it's your road map and your compass, all rolled into one. The business plan is going to tell you where you are, where you're going, and what your goal is.

In the first section, we will look at putting together a **professional business plan** in order to gain financing from a bank or lender. This is a portfolio similar to a resume with financial projections and other information for the bank to consider in order to grant you a loan.

In the second section of this chapter, we will talk about your own **personal business goals** in what you hope to accomplish in your business. We'll talk about how to set goals that are achievable and measurable.

Setting business goals will keep you motivated when you're feeling down or lost, and help you stay focused and end up with a successful business that makes you money and brings you joy.

What is a Professional Business Plan?

This section deals with how to outline your Business Plan in a portfolio – similar to a resume with financial projections and other information – that you will present to the bank in order for them to consider granting you a business loan.

It's imperative that you write a good business plan. This is the most vital piece of paper that you can produce if you're looking to buy a business and/or get financing for your business.

Not only does a business plan help you get favorable financing, but it also gives you a clear outline of what and how your business needs to operate.

Your business plan should outline how you will be able to improve business in the near future and generate more profit.

How to Write a Business Plan

First, since you are presenting this plan to a bank, presentation says a lot about your professionalism. You want a nice looking binder and cover page, since your full plan will be about 10 to 20 pages long.

Once you write up the plan, you can take it to a Staples or Office Max to have them put it together nicely in a binder. You may want to include labeled tabs or a table of contents if it is quite long.

What Goes Inside Your Business Plan

Here is what you should include inside the folder, in this order:

Cover letter

You must write a cover letter addressed to the lending officer, the person in charge of commercial lending. Really do try to find out who this is so that you can address it to them by name.

That way you are making your case to an individual and not broad audience or an impersonal institution. It makes you appear more educated and intentional, and is just professional courtesy. Typically you can address your letter to the person in charge of commercial lending.

Make it a precise summary of what you are trying to achieve. Here is an example of a business cover letter for applying for a loan:

Joanne Smith

123 Oak Ave, Dayton, OH 12345 ♦ 800-888-8888 ♦ jsmith@yahoo.com

January 1, 2021

Mr. Bill Woodley
Wells Fargo
123 Maple Ave
Cincinnati, OH 12345

Dear Mr. Woodley,

I, Joanne Smith with Greystones LLC, am seeking to purchase the filling station at 112 Main St, Dayton, OH. I am looking to get a loan of $300,000, as I already have $50,000 on hand.

I am looking to get financing with a favorable business rate and am providing my convenience store at 222 First St, Dayton, OH, as collateral.

Thank you for your consideration and looking over the enclosed business plan.

Sincerely,

Joanne Smith

Joanne Smith

Enclosure: Business Plan

As you can see, you want to quickly tell the lender who you are, why you are requesting a loan, the amount of the loan, how much financing you already have, and what collateral you can offer. Then thank them for reviewing your business plan.

Remember, the purpose of a Business Plan is to forecast a good idea, financial goals, and how you want to get there. You are essentially showing how you will make money and pay back the bank loan. You want to be thorough and professional. Here are the nine main parts of a solid business plan.

9 Parts of a Business Plan

After the cover letter, your business plan should have nine parts:

1. Mission statement

These are the objectives you are trying to achieve by buying or acquiring that business.

Example:

My goal is to provide the community with the best customer service and the best product at the best possible prices.

2. Executive summary

Your Executive Summary should have three things: Who you are, your startup summary, and your business objectives.

    a. **Who you are:** A detailed statement of who you or your partners are. If you have partners, then you need to identify each individual by name, what type of experience they have, with some explanation but not too much detail.

Example:

John Smith has been in the gas station industry for xx years, and he has successfully increased sales in xxx

    b. **Startup summary:** These are the basics: What business or location you are looking to buy. All the things you mentioned in your cover letter: Your purchase price, negotiated down payment, how much you need financing for, and collateral for this loan amount.

    3. **Objectives:** What you are trying to achieve by obtaining this business or location

Example:

My objectives are: To capture and increase a share of local commuter traffic passing through [a particular area]. To offer customers superior products. To provide excellent customer service. To solve a certain problem or meet a certain need.

4. Company overview

Give details about the company you already formed and are operating. Include these:

a. Name and location. If LLC or S Corp or C Corp, etc. What my company has done so far. If you are sole prop or if you have 20% ownership, etc.

b. Who are owners If multiple locations, mention all locations and owners.

c. Mention expertise of company, how long established, how much experience

d. Management team, who has what type of jobs/duties. Who handles finance, management, sales. Identify them individually.

e. Product and services

Keep in mind that the lender wants to know that you have the experience in the same field that you are purchasing a business, for those particular products and services, and if it's relevant to the venture you are seeking funds to undertake.

5. Operational plan

These are the final details of the plan. Lenders want you to explain what you are planning to do in the new business, and how it will operate.

a. Location: The business address.

b. Competitors: What is your direct competition like in the nearby vicinity, maybe a 2-3 mile radius. Analyze what they sell and what makes you stand out.

Do a "Competitive Analysis" that points out the strategic strength and positioning that you have over your competitors. Maybe your entrance is easier to access, maybe you have better brands or products, or you are closer to a busy intersection. Build a case for your own business. Point out advantages that you will have over your competition.

6. **Target market**

   a. Demographics: If this is a retail or brick-and-mortar store, look at the area: the demographics of the people who live there. You can find this information easily from government data: males to females, age, median income, white collar, etc. You'll want to explore your target market because you need to build a case that you are looking to attract this segment of people by offering this product or service.

   b. Market needs: Explain whether the business is in a busy market or rural market, and how that plays into what type of need you are meeting.

   For example, is there a large population of migrant farm workers who prefer a unique line of drinks and snacks that no one else carries?

Or do you have a lot of boaters in the area who need non-ethanol fuel?

Pay attention to market needs, and explain how you are doing that. What do your potential customers want that no one else is offering—that you will supply for them?

7. Marketing plan

a. Your competitive position: Where do you stand among your competitors?

b. Pricing strategy and profit margins.

c. Promotional strategies: What specials and offers you will use to draw in sales.

d. Sales forecast for the current year and next two years.

SMART Goals

An important element to creating a successful business plan is having the right goals. What is the difference between a good goal and a poor goal?

There are actually several important facets to defining your goals. If you don't make the proper goals or take these things into consideration, it can be very hard to achieve your goals.

What do I mean? For one, a good goal is clear an achievable. Be specific and realistic. Take a moment and think about realistic goals you have for the future that can be reasonably achieved.

BE SPECIFIC AND REALISTIC.

In fact, there is a tool used in the corporate business world that works well for the small business owner. Let me share it with you and see if it is useful to you.

Have you heard of SMART goals? SMART is an acronym, and it's used in the business world to help you set and achieve your goals. It stands for:

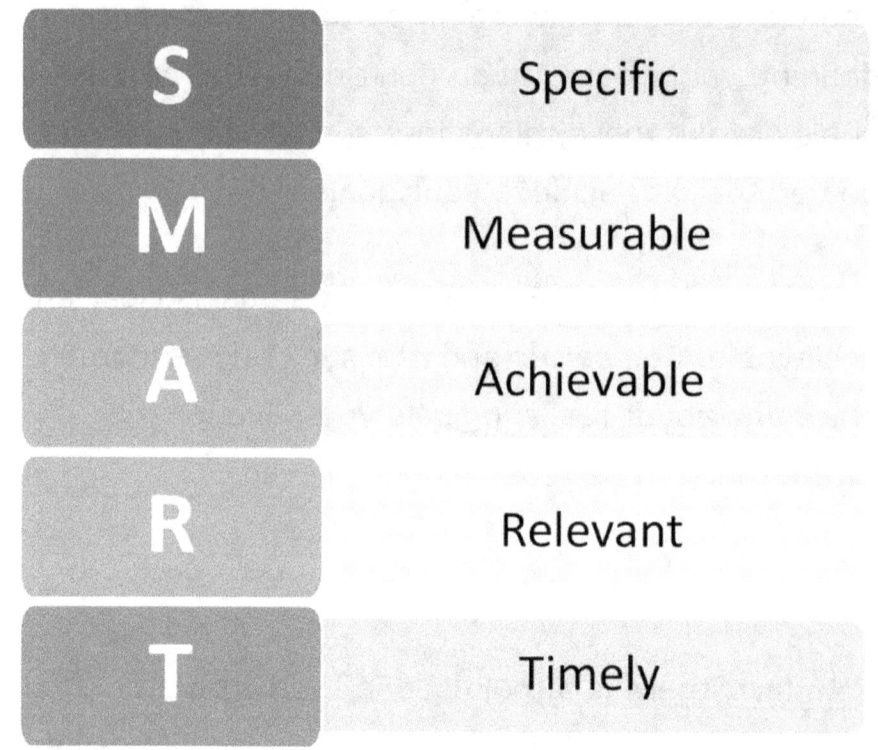

Each goal you make for your business should be SMART. It should be specific, not vague. Measurable, not flexible. Achievable, not unrealistic. Relevant, not something completely out of left field. And timely, meaning that you have a set date – six weeks, six months, next year, whenever is realistic and achievable.

Are you with me so far? Okay, let's break it down piece by piece.

Creating a Specific Goal

What are your specific goals? What do you hope to achieve in your business? You may say:

"I want to be a millionaire."

"I want to make enough to live on the beach."

"I want to quit my job."

Although these are all great goals, they just aren't specific enough. How can you make your goals so specific that you will immediately know when you achieve them? Dig deeper. You need to really think about the following list of questions:

- What is it that you want to accomplish?
- What do you wish to make happen?
- Where can you make this goal a reality?
- Who is going to be involved in the success of your goal?
- Why is this goal important to you?

For every goal you set, ask yourself these questions, and write down the answers in bullet-point form. If you can't answer these questions for each goal you're setting yourself, then your goal is not specific enough. Dig deeper.

Creating a Measurable Goal

This one is a little easier to achieve than your 'specific' goal, but it is so important that your goals are measurable and realistic. If you can't measure your goals, how do you know when you've hit one?

With each goal, ask yourself: How much? How many? How and when will I know this goal is accomplished and I've succeeded? Once you know the very specifics of your goal like this, you know it's measurable. If you can't answer these questions, go back to the drawing board and take another look at your goals.

Creating an Achievable Goal

Becoming a millionaire from your business is definitely shooting for the moon, but it isn't really an achievable goal at the start. Don't get me wrong, I'm not doubting your ability to get there eventually! But maybe hit a more immediately achievable goal, first.

For example:

"Make $1,000 in profit by x date" is a good, achievable goal.

"Streamline the system to allow the creation of x and y number of products per hour/day." This is a good, measurable, possible goal.

On the other hand, "Become nationally recognized," "Ship millions of shoes," or "Be inspiring" aren't great goals. You can't measure them, and you probably can't attain them—at least not the first two.

Creating a Relevant Goal

Is this goal appropriate, realistic, and in line with who you are and what you can accomplish? Does it meet a need for/speak to your customers?

Think about your target market and the world at large. What is relevant to that? Extreme, rapid expansion might not be relevant or possible within a down economy or in a tough area. Expanding your business and moving into a new workshop within the year might not be a relevant goal when you've got plenty of space right now, and need that money to go to other things.

A relevant goal is worthwhile, matches/supports your other goals, and most of all, matches you and your business. Your goals should always be relevant not only to you but also to your business as a whole.

Creating a Timely Goal

Timely, or time-based, goals are so important! When there is no time frame attached to your goal, there is no urgency or concern. Set dates and times you wish to complete your goals, and follow through to the best of your abilities.

"Ship x number of figurines" is a fine goal, but with no time limit, it falls flat. Instead, "ship x amount of figurines by y date" is more focused and specific.

When looking at timeframes, consider: When will it be done? What can I do today, tomorrow, and this week? What can be done in six weeks? What do I need to accomplish by the end of this quarter/this year?

The more specific you are, the better. Be realistic and hold yourself to your own standards.

When you put all of these things together, then you will have SMART goals—attainable and relevant to your business. Each goal that you lay out for your business needs to go through the SMART goal frame of reference. If one of your goals fails one of these questions, go back to the drawing board and be more specific.

That way, you know what your target is. You know what to aim for. And you will know when you have achieved your goals.

Chapter 6 – Excellent Employees

You can have the best business plan, products, and competitive prices—but if you don't have a good person behind the counter interacting with customers, your business just isn't going to thrive.

Do you have employees? Or is your business growing to the point where you need to consider hiring a full-time or part-time employee or two? You can outsource some things (marketing, accounting, branding), but there will come a point that you need to hire regular employees.

Finding the right employees is absolutely critical to your business's success. As I said, you can have the best of all the other aspects (products, prices)—but without the right people interacting with your customers, you won't be able to sell anything. They are the face of your business.

The right staffing is a very important key to your business's short- and long-term success. Don't simply hire the first person that walks through your door, or your friends, or a cousin or a niece. Make sure you're getting the best help that you can. It can make or break your business, believe me.

I'd like to share with you my process for finding the right employees, training them, and including them in special promotions so that sales will increase and employee motivation will go up. It's a rewards system that really works in a retail business. I'll also talk about some common staff issues and how to solve them.

10 Steps to Successful Staffing

We're going to talk about where to look for the right employees; how to interview, train, retain, and motivate them; how to take care of bad behavior; and how to involve them in some useful promotions that will benefit you and your staff.

How to Find the Right Staff

I am sure every one of us has walked into a store with a notice on the front door that says "Now Hiring." Seems harmless enough, right? In my opinion, this is not a good idea. Why? Well, your target audience, in this case, is your surrounding neighborhood, so most of the applications that you will get are from the neighborhood.

Let's say you get ten applications, and you meet and interview each of them, and end up hiring one person out of the ten. Chances are, you may alienate the other nine; as a result, some of those people who were your customers at first may not come back afterward simply because you didn't hire them.

The best practice is to hire people through advertising in a way that covers your city or locality and not just your neighborhood. I have three suggestions on where to advertise and find people.

A. **Run an ad on Craigslist.** You may be surprised how often people look for jobs on Craigslist. Craigslist is an essential tool for a lot of things, from selling your old couch to hiring people to do your yard work or carpentry work to hiring new employees. I use Craigslist every time I need help. Once I even hired an excellent bookkeeper from there. Of course you need to screen these applicants well, and I'll talk about the interview process.

B. **Word of mouth.** You can ask some of your other employees if they know of any competent and decent people they can recommend. Ask your friends or other business owners that you know well; this way you, at least, have a reference where they are coming from.

C. **Hiring employees from local retailers.** This sounds bad I know; but again remember, you are not doing anything illegal or unethical. There is a right way to do it. Let me explain. You go to your local burger joint, and the lady who took your order was very courteous and professional. Strike up a conversation with her, compliment her on her professionalism, let her know you own such and such business, and you are looking to hire some decent employees.

Ask her if she knows anyone that she can recommend. Give her your business card. You will see that, out of five people you meet this way, three will call you either with a recommendation or they will call to apply for themselves. There are three reasons she may contact you. First, obviously people love compliments; second, most employees do not feel appreciated enough at their current jobs; and third, everyone wants to move up at their job and eventually make more money. So take advantage of that; you never know if you are a better fit.

Now that you have some applicants calling you, you need to give them each an application, right? Where do you get these job applications? I am sure you can go to the local office supply store and pick up a stack of forms, but is that a good idea? The answer is no. Those applications are very generic and not designed for your type of business.

So it's best to create one or modify an existing one you may already have that fits your needs. You can also go to my blog, (GasStationBusiness101.com) and find a generic job application under the Resource tab that you can download and modify it to meet your own specific needs.

When preparing a job application, here are a few things to keep in mind:

Absolutely *do not* ask for a social security number on the application. It is also a good idea not to ask about race on a job application.

Make sure to ask about their education level, previous employment history, and how many addresses they've had in the last five years. These three things can tell you a lot about a person. If an applicant held one job for the last five years, lived in one address in the past five years and had a high school education – chances are better that he or she will be a good employee. In general, this is true, compared to an applicant that had four jobs in the last five years, moved three times in that same period, and does not have a high school diploma.

When asking about previous employment, make sure to ask the name and contact information of the company along with the name of their supervisors. This way you can check their references.

Remember, it is a common practice for employers not to reveal any details of a current or former employee for legal reasons. So if you ask if they were they good or bad at their job, you may not get an answer, you may just have to read between the lines (or *hear* in this case). A better question to ask, which they can answer freely, is whether that person could be rehired or not. If they say he or she can be rehired, you know they are saying they do recommend that person as an employee. If they say no, then there is some reason why. It's a red flag.

Asking the Right Interview Questions

Once you find some decent applicants, call a few of them for an interview. What should you ask them? Consider the role they will have.

For those who will be handling money, I always give them a simple math test to see if they can calculate basic addition and subtraction in their heads. It is a good idea to ask a few hypothetical questions ranging from how to handle a customer service issue to an emergency situation. If someone were to get sick inside the store, how would they handle that emergency?

Watch and listen to see if they use a common sense approach in their answers. If they will be handling stock or even large trash bags, I ask them if they have any physical limitations which may prevent them from performing the normal duties and responsibilities of the store's work – specifically, if they are able to pick up 30 pounds or not.

Remember, heavy lifting is important, as any typical gas station's garbage can may weigh as much as 25-30 pounds, so it is important to know if they can or not. But remember, you cannot discriminate if they cannot lift that weight; but as long as you know they can't, you can arrange someone else on the schedule to pick that trash up.

Next, I usually ask if they can bring a **background check** of themselves from the local police dept, and I do offer to pay for that cost. It saves money and time to have them provide you with that report instead of you running a background check on them.

Once all of these things check out, go ahead and hire them. One more thing to make clear right before you hire them: Let them know that it is your company policy to hire people with a 60- to 90-day probation period. Meaning, they can be let go anytime during those 60 to 90 days without giving them any reasons based on their performance.

Once you hire them, there is some basic paperwork that you need to have them fill out and keep it in their employee file. I am sure everyone of you that is in business has a set of paperwork that you keep for your new hires. But I would still like to go through a checklist of some of the paperwork I keep on file for each of my new hires so you can match it with yours.

- The completed job application that you already have

- W-2 from the IRS

- A disclaimer about the 60 to 90-day probation period (In it, I explain for the next 60 to 90 days they are on probation, their job can be terminated based on poor performance, and I have them sign it.)

- Their criminal background check that they brought, keep it in their personnel file

- Copy of their social security card and driver's license or state identification card

- Store key responsibility agreement, if they will be given a key to the store. (In this one-page acknowledgment consent form, I want each employee to sign stating that they understand the true responsibility of safeguarding the store key. Also, it states that they will be responsible if they lose the key or it comes up missing.)

If they ask for a copy of any of the above, it's fine to provide it for them. Also, make sure that you give them any training resources they may need to take home. For example, a **new hire handbook** may be required. If you are a branded station or franchise, your parent company usually provides you with some basic training material to hand out to each new hire.

Remember some states require you to register all new employees you hire with the Department of Labor within seven days of hiring. If not, there will be a fine imposed on you. So check with your state's DOL and see if they require it. One more thing you need to find out is if your state is an "employment at will" state or not.

Alabama, among many other states, is an employment at will state. Meaning you can terminate anyone anytime without giving them any reason. Yes, it sounds odd I know, and maybe I am oversimplifying it, but the essence is that you really do not have to give them much of a reason for the termination. If your state is not, there may be laws about how you inform them of termination, reasons why, or time requirements.

Providing Proper Training

Once you hire an employee, it is important to provide them with proper training. First, give them a walk around the store and show them what you sell, how to stock it, and how to merchandise the items. Then show them how to restock the shelves and the coolers and how often that should be done.

It is a good idea to have a **checklist** that you can hand them which details their job duties and responsibilities, what is expected of them before they start their shift and after they close their shift. I usually provide three full days of training before I let any new employee work or run a shift all by themselves.

The first day, I show them around with the checklist. Then I put them with an experienced cashier so they can observe the operation of the cash register for at least two hours without touching the register at all. The second half of that day, I let them get more hands-on training where they will start doing the transaction while the trainer stands next to them and guides them through each step.

The second day, I again explain the checklist and let them do the pre-shift chores (which usually involves restocking the coolers before taking over the shifts, making sure the fountain and coffee area is fully stocked, etc.) Then they do a shift again with a trainer, but today they have to take the lead while the trainer stands next to them. They are allowed to ask questions but are to do all the work themselves.

The third day, they will be totally on their own. There is a trainer on site but not next to them. Instead, I tell the trainer to go do other things away from the checkout stand so they can observe the new hire from a distance and see how they are doing. The new hire is only allowed to call the trainer when he or she is completely stuck.

After the third day is complete, I evaluate. Judging by how well the new hire did, we decide if they need one extra day of training, or if they are ready to go on their own. On rare occasions, after the second or third day of training, either the new hire decides not to work anymore, or we decide that this person won't be able to handle this task or the job.

Once we know that fact, we do not continue the training. Instead, we just tell them it will not work while explaining to them the reasons we didn't think they are a good fit for our store. Since they already signed the probation agreement, it is not a legal issue at all.

Employee Appearance

Appearance is the most important first impression on your customer. You do not get a second chance to create that first impression, so make sure your employees are in a uniform of some sort. If you are a branded store like Shell, BP, Chevron, or a franchise, then you have a uniform that you provide your employees along with a name tag.

> YOU DON'T GET A SECOND CHANCE TO MAKE A FIRST IMPRESSION ON YOUR CUSTOMERS.

But what if you are a non-branded store? You can still get some uniform for them. Go to your local screen printing store, and you can get t-shirts with your logo and name printed on them for a very nominal price. One quick note on that: If you don't have a logo for your store, you can go online to Fiverr.com and pay $5 and get a logo created for you. There is no reason not to be professional. Make sure your store and employees look just as professional as branded store employees.

A good first impression is priceless. And a uniform helps your employees remember they represent you.

Motivating & Empowering Your Staff

You need to make sure your employees do not feel that this is a dead end job. To do so, you need to motivate them. Typically, there are three ways that you can motivate your employees.

1. **By showing them the ladder** they can climb to be a manager one day. From the cashier, to shift leader, to shift manager to assistant manager, and then finally store manager one day. Let them know that it is possible with hard work and dedication.

2. **Tell them how you increase their pay.** I typically tell all new hires that I will start them at a certain hourly rate; then after 60 days they will get a raise to a certain hourly rate. Every six months I will

do a performance review of them, and if I see they are performing well, they will get a raise. You can tell them it will be every nine months or every three months. It is totally up to you.

3. **Compliments.** Another great way to motivate your staff is just simply by telling them they are doing a great job. Give them a compliment when you see good work, acknowledge it, and show them you noticed. A simple "thank you," or a pat on the back can go a long way sometimes. Remember, everybody wants to feel appreciated and valued. Especially those who do work extra hard or go the extra mile – and those staff members are worth their weight in gold.

Teaching Them Marketing 101

In this step, your team needs to know your marketing strategy so they can promote your store and certain products. Employees sharing promotions with your customers in person is very valuable.

Let me explain: Say you have a special on 2-liter soda for 99 cents this month. If you want to promote it, it needs little more than a sign on the back of the store. Think if your employee mentioned this to each of the clients this week or this month: "We have 2-liters of soda for 99 cents today." Two out of five customers may buy that; it is that simple.

Another example: Say you have a two-pack cigarette special where you give a lighter for free. Ask your employees to mention that to anyone buying a single pack of cigarettes.

See how many of them end up buying two packs instead; you will be surprised. More than 50% will go for the two-pack special. Face-to-face marketing can be a very powerful thing.

Rewarding Good Behavior

If you see an employee doing a great job handling a bad situation at work, or they showed some exceptional quality or ability which is beyond their daily work duties and responsibilities, reward them. At least acknowledge their work or effort. Buy them lunch, or sit down and have lunch with him or her; it can mean a lot to them. Give them a gift certificate for a movie or pizza. Even something small like that can make them feel appreciated and proud of being a part of your team. It helps build a good, solid workforce overall.

How to Discipline Bad Behavior

Now let's face the truth: We don't always get the best employees. There are bad apples in every bunch, right? Now how do you discipline bad behavior when you see it? What I am talking about here is not doing their job properly, giving poor customer service, not doing their side work, or even showing up to work late more than once in the same week. Nothing too serious, but still it is poor performance. We'll talk about more serious issues in a moment.

For minor issues like I mentioned, you can give them a verbal warning first and monitor them to see if there is any improvement. If there is no change and they continue the bad behavior, you can then give them a written warning.

Most stores have these forms of written warnings where you fill in the specific improper action that they took or the job that they did not perform even after a prior verbal warning. Once you give them a copy of that, ask them to sign it and keep a copy of it in their personnel file. If he or she makes the same violation within 30 days of giving them the written warning, I usually terminate an employee.

What about if it is something more serious? If you encounter truly bad behavior—theft, bullying, violating company policy, or refusing to perform their job—these are grounds for immediate termination and not a disciplinary action.

Goal-Oriented Incentives

Something that is a great win-win for both me and my employees is running occasional special incentive programs. They get rewarded for making certain goals; this is incredibly motivating.

I do this often in my stores. I set up individual goals and offer incentives if they reach the goal. For example: I had a store with a car wash, and prices were set at $2 for basic, $4 for the medium grade wash and $7 for the works, the ultimate wash. I set up a plan where every time a cashier sold any of the medium level wash they would get $.50 cents, and if they sold any $7 wash, I would pay them $1 for each wash sold.

As long as they kept each receipt and signed their name on the ticket, every week I would pay them. Before this incentive program, my monthly car wash sales were around $2,000 a month.

Once I started it, from the very next month, my carwash sales rose to around $3,500 to as high as $5,400 one month. It was well worth it for me and for them!

You can be very creative when it comes to creating an incentive program, but it depends on what you sell in your store.

I have done the same with deli food, where I set up a daily target and a weekly target, and if they reached that goal, each employee got an incentive bonus payment.

To be specific, I was making $6,500 a week on deli revenue; I told them if we could get the weekly revenue to $9,000 a week, then I would pay each employee $75. That was also a fast success and helped them all to be motivated at work.

Those incentive programs don't have to be done every week; you can alternate weeks or change it. One week it's deli food; later it's soda sales. It's a great way to boost morale—and when you do, you also raise sales and improve customer service.

> BOOSTING EMPLOYEE MORALE IMPROVES CUSTOMER EXPERIENCE.

Regular Employee Meetings & Coaching

Last but not least, it is very important to have regularly scheduled employee meetings and coaching. Meet every month, where you tell them of any upcoming changes in your store, and then ask for any issues they faced that month or any concerns they have.

This is also the time to roll out any new incentive plans you have for them for the following month. Tell them about new incentive programs and how they will work.

Offer them tips, words of encouragement, and remind them to greet and make eye contact with each customer. Also, emphasize the restroom cleaning regime and keeping the coffee and fountain areas clean. We all tend to forget things, and being refreshed helps.

CHAPTER 7 – SELLING SECRETS: FIVE PROVEN WAYS TO INCREASE SALES

After 26+ years in various retail small businesses, I've picked up some valuable insight that I'd like to share with you about increasing sales.

Actually, I wrote a whole book, *Sales Genie,* in which I go into detail about several ways to boost retail sales. Here, I'll attempt to summarize the majority of my book into one quick and useful chapter for you. But if you find sales are your biggest pain point, you may want to get that book. (It's free on Audible and only a few dollars on Kindle.)

The good news is, there are many things you can do to increase your sales. For a few years, my gas station businesses were so successful that a large oil company hired me to turn around their unprofitable service stations. I was able to turn nine businesses around. The sales increased from 20% to as high as 60% in some stores. I mastered a simple yet proven method that I created to improve those businesses.

These are my top 5 selling strategies, learned over the years. So let's start!

1 - Product Merchandising & Pricing

First, you need to get the right products. What are they? Well, that depends on your customer base. I talked about this earlier—supplying ethanol fuel to boaters, etc. As I mentioned, look around: Who are your customers, and what do they want?

If you're a brick-and-mortar store, selecting the right products based on your immediate neighborhood clientele is key to your success.

Remember it is the products that you carry which attract people to your store. If a customer knows you carry a certain type of bread or tobacco that is not carried by your competitor, then yes, he or she will come to your store regularly to shop with you.

A Tale of 3 Stores

Now, I want you to really get the picture here. I will take three convenience stores in three vastly different neighborhoods and talk about how their product selections may vary from one to the other. Let's assume:

- Store 1 is an ethnically mixed inner city location
- Store 2 is in a rural countryside location
- Store 3 is in the fancy part of town

First, let's take store one. In the cigarette category you will carry more varieties of menthol type cigarettes, and then on the tobacco side, you will carry a selection of single cigars. In the beer and wine side, you will carry more of a certain type of beer and wine that are mostly sold in a single can or bottle than your other store in the rural area.

Similarly, your grocery selection will vary widely too. In this store you may have to carry canned meat that is ready to eat; in the candy section, you will notice more of a selection of the candies that are less than a $1.00 each or sometimes bags of candy that are two for $1.00.

Now let's do the same for store 2 in the rural area. In this store your cigarettes will be mostly non-menthol, full flavored cigarettes that are subgeneric brands, as for tobacco, you will notice you sell mostly generic can tobacco and not much of single cigars. So you have to make room to put more of a selection of those in this store.

As for beer and wine, you will see that you sell mostly bigger packages of cheaper beer like suitcases or eighteen-packs and not much of the smaller packages like six-packs. Similarly, all other product categories will be a little different than the previous one.

Now as for store 3 in the fancy part of town, your cigarette and tobacco sales will be different again. Here you may see you sell mostly high-value branded cigarettes like Marlboro and such; and for tobacco, you will notice you sell the branded tobacco and good quality cigars.

On the beer side, you will notice you sell mostly high-end six-pack premium or imported beer versus generic cheaper beers. Same goes for wine; you will see that you sell a lot of $15 or higher valued wine bottles in this store. In grocery, you will sell mostly premium candy and gum and not much of the $1.00 value candies.

So as you can see, there is no cookie-cutter setup that fits every store; it is unique for each location and each business.

No cookie-cutter setup fits every store.

Pro tip: Part of this improvement process is talking and getting feedback from your customers. It is a good idea to keep a log handy so that every time a customer asks for something or looks for items you don't carry, write them down so you can order them next time and let the customer know that you will carry the item just for them. This can make a customer feel important and valued; and trust me, he or she will be a loyal customer to your store for years to come.

This is the kind of above-and-beyond mentality that will draw customers away from your competitors to shop loyally with you. And it's a pleasure to do business this way, in my opinion.

Vendors can be a great resource. Ask them what sells well in your particular neighborhood and order based on their recommendation. Remember, if you sell more, then you'll buy more—and that's a win-win for you both. Also, compare prices from the grocery suppliers that are available to you. There are national chains, regional companies, and local companies.

Also, if you haven't already done so, check out your competitors. How are they displaying their products? What are they stocking? It may give you some valuable insight.

Three-month check-up

Finally, this step is very important: After you purchase or arrange the merchandise in your store based on your research, you're not done. You have to give it three months and then analyze your sales and go back and change things that need improvement.

What you are trying to find out now is the sales per square foot. To figure this number out first, you need to know the square foot size of your sales floor and not the whole store. So if you had $70,000 in sales the previous month, and you have 1400 square feet of sales floor, your sales per square foot are 70,000/1400 = 50. So your sales per square foot per month was $50.

Next, look through your shelves and merchandising, try to find items that are slow moving—items that you order once a month or less. Remove them and try similar items to replace them. Similarly, if you notice you are ordering some items every week and still running out, give them more visibility and room by giving them two shelf spaces instead of one. This way you are increasing the exposure of some of the high sellers.

Wait three months and calculate your sales per square foot again, and see if it increased or not.

A typical rule of thumb is if your reorder frequency is six to eight weeks for most merchandise, then it is considered a slow seller.

Your best bet would be to replace it with another item or just remove it altogether. Remember, every time you remove an item like that and replace it with a faster moving/selling item, your sales per square foot goes up. In return, your profit goes up, so you make more money overall.

Make sure to read the section on Penny Profit and Profit Margin to understand how pricing works best.

If you buy from a grocery company, many times they will pre-price items based on your requested profit margin. This is the profit margin I tell my grocery company to price my merchandise at:

- Grocery at 35%

- Candy at 40%
- Automotive Accessories & oil at 50%
- Drinks at 37%
- Tobacco at 25%
- Deli food at 50%
- Cigarettes at 17%

2 - STAFF

Sales is directly impacted by your staff. Have you ever walked out of a store because no one was willing to help you, or even just take your money? Make no mistake, you can have the best products at great prices, but you need the right person there to sell it and interact with your customers to succeed.

Make sure you read the previous chapter in which I talk about having excellent employees. It's not the luck of the draw. You as the employer need to find, hire, train, and retain the right people. Check out my step by step process to follow for all your staffing needs.

Proper staffing is one of the vital keys to your success. And to your sales and profits.

You might ask yourself: Who is your best employee? Do you reward them? Do the others see their example and have a reason to follow it? Selling your products is their job; motivating them is yours.

3 - MARKETING & PROMOTIONS

In this 21st century, marketing and promotion for brick-and-mortar businesses have changed a whole lot. It's not all about just in-store or local area marketing; it is about online marketing too. That's why I have an entire section about Social Media Marketing. Make sure you read it and give some of those strategies a try.

Any retail store operator understands the importance of marketing. Unless you are reaching out to your target audience, how can you expect them to become customers? However, for that to happen, it is important to understand about local area marketing and using the right tactics and techniques. Local area marketing can help you to create local buzz and interest for your store. Good marketing requires constant effort to attract people to you, as well as understanding your local community and target market.

4 Local Area Promotion Ideas

Organize an Event

Whether it is an awareness session or an annual sale, events are a great way for the community to gather to generate interest in your business. It also provides a great opportunity for the business executives to meet their customers and allow them to know you better. Today, business is more about relationships, and if you are not able to maintain healthy relationships with your customers, then you can wave them off to your competitor.

To develop trust with customers and the community takes time. Another idea is to sponsor any local event in your area, such as a local school kids' baseball, football, or softball games. Cater some food and drinks for a Sunday service at your local church. Typically, these types of sponsorships do not cost much but get your name out there as a productive member of your local community.

Create Partnerships

A business can also build partnerships with other local businesses or non-business organizations to become active and get noticed in the local community. It will help give a boost to your company, and you can also participate in local community events this way.

For example, a business can collaborate with the local school program or function where they can play an active and productive role. If the parents are your target customers and they will be present at the event, then this can be a great way to raise awareness of your business while doing some good for the community.

Personal Introductions

If you want to grow your local influence, another good strategy, which is also becoming increasingly popular among entrepreneurs, is personal introductions. Make it a point to introduce your business to at least five people each week in person. Whether it is in your store, at the local bar or another place where you know your target audience is likely to hang out. Giving them your business card is an effective marketing strategy.

When you can form a relationship with someone at a personal level, chances are they are more likely to shop at your store or at least try it out. If they like it, they are more likely to refer other people to it. So suppose you meet 250 new people in a year, chances are at least 50 of them will become your customer or spread the word about your business to others.

By personally putting yourself out there, you are giving them an opportunity to talk about you. Even if they don't become your customer, they are likely to tell others about their encounter with you and in doing so; they will end up talking about your business or store.

Offer Exclusive Discounts

If your store is located somewhere near a major employer, you can offer discounts or offers to their employees. This is also a good way to generate local buzz because that way you are not only targeting local employees but also their families. You may be offering a discount only to them, but they are more likely to bring their family over as well if they have a positive experience with your brand.

Making the local employees your VIP customer is also a good strategy. By distributing VIP discount cards through the employer for their employees, you can enhance your chances of being paid a visit by those who haven't tried your store out before.

If you know a local event or carnival is taking place, you can hand out your company brochures or offer discounts as a way to attract people. Even a minimal discount could mean that you will, at least, attract some part of that audience which you were targeting. Marketing strategies don't take a lot of time, but they require constant action and attention.

Be sure to check out the chapter on social media marketing, as well as the section on in-store promotions in the chapter on profit. Also, consider starting an email list where you send monthly specials to those on your list. You can sign customers up in your store by offering them discounts; this builds relationships and business.

4 - STREAMLINING COSTS & EXPENSES

It is crucial to learn how to manage your money and cut down on unnecessary expenses. The very first place to start is the **bank**. Obtain your bank analysis statement which has a breakdown of your basic service charges, and study them carefully to find out where you can cut down. Talk to your banker if you need to understand how you can reduce your bank costs.

Invest in **good accounting software**. If you are not evaluating your costs and expenses on an automated system, it is unlikely that you will be efficient with your money. Companies that don't invest in good accounting software also face difficulty at tax or audit time. (See more in the Legal Matters chapter about accounting and software.)

What are your **benchmarks**? How do you compare with the competition? Use industry benchmarks to evaluate your costs and expenses to understand where you may be underspending or overspending. Every industry is unique.

Audit yourself. Studying the incoming and outgoing revenue carefully can help highlight costs that are too high, areas where your business has dipped in revenue, and other costs that can be controlled. Keep good records. If you don't keep careful track of your revenue and expenses, how can you make it more efficient.

Operating costs are another thing that you can streamline. Do you have an energy-efficient heating system, or is there a way to cut your utility costs? What about travel costs – are some aspects of the job that could be done at home or online?

Let me share some examples here: I saved $900 a month by using LED lighting and changing some fixtures in one store. I also had my A/C serviced, and the tech advised me on how to save on my power bill. I followed his advice (some things as simple as a lock box on the thermostat, changing A/C filters, cleaning the vent hood filters on the fryers weekly, adding thermostat controlled exhaust fans, etc.). I invested $1,000 in his changes, and saw a savings of $400 a month from that alone.

Other things you can do to save on your monthly operating costs: Put your faucets and toilets on an auto shut-off system to save on water; shop around to reduce monthly charges for phone, internet, and trash pickup.

Streamline inventory. Can you improve your stocking system or streamline your inventory? Are there some products that sell better than others?

Vendor negotiation. Conduct productive vendor negotiations to get the best possible rates/prices on your purchased items every year. Be aware of the current price rate in the market, review the trends, and study the market conditions. You can also get their input on what are the best selling products so that they can sell more and so can you.

5 - MINIMIZING THEFT & ERRORS

Most small and large retailers end up losing around 1%-2% of their total sales in theft by both customers and by employees, mishandling of inventory, and various errors.

As a small business owner, if you pay attention to a few things, you can save money and make your business run lean and mean. Remember, regardless of how well your merchandising or pricing is, if people are stealing from you, chances are you won't see much of profit from all your hard work.

Now, it is hard to stop theft completely. If we want to be realistic, we should try to control theft and not expect to eliminate it entirely.

The two types of theft are external and internal. External theft is done by people from outside – often customers or vendors stealing from you. There are a few steps you can take to deter stealing.

Steps to Defer External Theft

1. Identify merchandise that can be easily stolen
2. Change your layout so high-risk merchandise can be better monitored by employees
3. Focus your video cameras on weak areas
4. Install a video monitor where both your cashiers and customers can see them
5. Put a sign in the front window about video surveillance

6. Install two theft deterrent convex mirrors around the back of your store
7. Limit how many kids can enter the store at one time (only if you are in a school zone)
8. Train employees to make eye contact with customers as soon as they walk in

Preventing Vendor Theft

I once had a vendor who was taking bottles of soda out of the middle of the cases. I accidentally caught him one day, and the company ended up sending me 120 cases of product that they estimated he had stolen in the previous four months.

Make sure your employees check the shipments and take their time. If you need to, set rules for when vendors can come to ensure an employee will be free to check the shipments.

Preventing Internal Theft

Every dollar you lose due to theft, twenty cents of that was done by outsiders, and eighty cents was done by your own people.

In the retail world, there are a few different ways employees can steal at work:

- Doing refunds and voids
- Not ringing up a sale
- Doing "sweetheart" deals
- Consuming products for their own use
- Taking merchandise home
- Being short on their shift paperwork
- "Riding the clock."

To set up a good defense against this, focus on items that are commonly stolen. For my convenience stores, it was cigarettes, beer, and deli food. So I set up a system where each employee had to do a cigarette inventory count at the beginning and end of their shift and match that with register sales.

Here are some other steps you can take:

- Video surveillance (only works if you watch from time to time)
- Cash register to video interface where all transactions get recorded
- Good hiring and background check process
- Having a functional inventory control system

- Periodic employee coaching and training
- Enforcing and monitoring clock in and out

No business wants to believe that their employees may be stealing, but if there are discrepancies in sales numbers, chances are you may have a problem which requires immediate action.

Fostering Loyalty

Let me say this, too: Committing to your employees in a positive way will drive employee loyalty. Provide them incentives and show that you care for them. An engaged employee is more likely to work for the progress of your company and not its downfall. Companies are starting to realize the importance of employee commitment and to use techniques to motivate them.

Focus on empowering and strengthening your employees so that they are loyal to you and work for the growth of your company.

4 Steps to Boost Sales 25% in 60 Days

Now it's time to set some specific goals that are attainable to get you to your target sales in two months doing exactly what I just outlined earlier. Here are four steps to get you there.

1. Product Refresh

The first week you need to focus on your product line and merchandising efforts. Follow those steps, tweak and fix what you need to fix in your merchandising lineup. Every time I took over a new business, this is what I would do the very first week, remerchandising the store with the right type of products and placing them where they belong.

Typically, I would do this just by remerchandising and bringing in more targeted products for that specific neighborhood. Week one, do your research about the neighborhood and identify your product lines that are well targeted towards your local market, then do a layout on a piece of paper of how you want the product displays to flow. Week two, you order the products, and in week three, you do the changes and all the actual remerchandising that you planned in the last two weeks.

In this same period, you can also implement everything that I mentioned under Pricing Strategy as well, remember, effective merchandising and effective pricing both go hand in hand and so you need to implement both at the same time. By doing this you will create a WOW factor in your store when customers walk in and see the new layout of your store, along with all the new products and it will only get better if you have great, and often times, lower prices to display on those products. Just these two changes alone can improve your sales by 5%-10%.

2. Employee Pep Talk

Next, you will need help from your employees. But before they can offer their help, you need to make sure you hire, train, coach, and empower them. Teach them the basics of Marketing 101 and make sure to reward them for the right behavior.

Remember, it's all about motivation. If you follow the steps properly, you should see an increase in your sales by at least 5%, maybe much more. If you start this process the first week, this will take you three weeks or a little more to complete and a month to see the positive results.

3. Promotions

Time to take a look at all the online and offline ways (event promotion, sponsoring the local school, church events, and games) I spoke about promoting your business. Remember those? If you try half of what we discussed, you should see an increase of 2%-5% in your business.

The biggest hike should come from all the internet or online efforts that you undertake. (See the Social

Media Marketing chapter.) In my experience, if you use sites like Facebook and collect email addresses, you should see an increase of at least 8%-10%.

So far, we have increased sales by at least 5% from item number one by implementing effective merchandising and pricing strategies.

The second increase of 5% comes from your employees. The third increase originates from all offline and online marketing efforts. Both combined is, at least, a 10% boost.

5% + 5% + 10% = 20%

Okay, so we have a little ways to go to get to our 25% sales boost goal. For this last 5%, we will have to take a different approach. Instead of boosting sales, we will reduce cost and expenses, so we end up with a savings that will translate into the same dollar value as if we increased sales by another 5%.

4. Reducing Costs

First, take the measures I discussed on how to save on operating expenses. Then take those steps to reduce theft and errors. These two things should translate into, at the very least, a 3% savings overall and it should not take more than five weeks to implement and see a difference.

Second, you should sit down and negotiate with all your vendors and see how you can get better pricing from them either by changing vendors or by buying bigger volume.

Typically, a good negotiation can result in savings of at least 2-3%. You can do this the very first or the second week and see some savings by the end of the second month, depending on how often you buy from them.

How did you do?

Did you get to your target of a 25% sales increase? I am confident that you will see improvement.

As for getting there in 60 days, most of these changes you can implement simultaneously, but it may take a few weeks to see the final results.

In my opinion, by the eighth week, you should be able to see all the positive results trickling down to your bank account.

CHAPTER 8 – SELLING ONLINE

Whether you are a brick-and-mortar shop, a private contractor who works from home, or a service provider—you will always have one thing in common. Your customers are online. That's why it's so important that you learn to sell online, or at least to interact with your customers online.

In this section, we will talk about your website, using social media, and the potential of online selling platforms. The internet is an amazing tool, and you need to use it to grow your business.

DO I NEED A WEBSITE?

Something I hear a lot from new business owners is the question: Do I really need a website? It seems like a lot of time, money, and commitment. Can't I just sell in person or on a platform?

The short answer is sure, you can. But nowadays, you still need a website.

Even if you're only planning on selling in person, a website is still quite a valuable tool. A good website tells consumers who you are, why they should care about your business, what products you sell, where they can purchase your products, and more.

Hopefully, you will even let your consumers buy directly *from* your website, so they can get access to your product whenever they want it. This is how many customers and clients prefer to do business, so if you don't have a website—you will be losing out on the business of a certain portion of clients.

Imagine how convenient it would be for someone – after they use the last of their favorite product made by you – to look at the label, see your website address, and simply go online and click a few keys to order more. Otherwise, how will they order more? Would they need to drive to your location, or wait until they are next in the area? You always want to make it easy for customers to buy from you.

A professional website with products, detailed descriptions, company information, and contact information also says a lot about you. Your professionalism, your trustworthiness. It makes your business seem more like a real, full-fledged resource for your customers. Even if you work from home or sell out of a shop, a website can (and probably will) bring in more business for you.

But Isn't a Website Expensive?

Isn't the cost prohibitive? It's not! I used to think this, too, but it's not at all. A domain name purchase should cost you less than $20 upfront, with an annual renewal of about $15 or so. Hosting is as cheap as $5/month, or even less in some places.

There are numerous different hosting websites, so shop around to make the right call for you. Sites like GoDaddy have a lot of advertising power backing them, but those who run the best ads aren't always the best choice for you.

Don't hesitate to ask other professionals who they use for their hosting needs and how much they pay.

Pro tip: You can certainly get a "free" domain from somewhere like Weebly or another site, but they will use their own extension at the end. Instead of *YourWebsite.com*, it will be *YourWebsite.Weebly.com*.

This does not make your website or your business seem very professional. It's tempting to go with the cheapest option at first, but if you spend a little more time and effort up front, it's pays off in the long run.

Personally, if I'm going to be making a purchase online or giving someone my credit card information, I'm looking for a high-quality website. I don't want to give my personal information to a website that seems cheap, questionable, or hastily thrown together.

Your website is your first impression for many people, and it's very important that you cultivate your online persona well.

Isn't Building a Website Hard?

It can feel overwhelming to create your own website if you haven't done it before, but it's not nearly as technical as it seems. WordPress has come a long way over the years, and installing WordPress to run on your website is just a handful of clicks. Whoever you use for hosting – Namecheap, Bluehost, etc. – should have detailed instructions that are pretty foolproof.

Once you've installed WordPress on your website, consider using a premade template, at least for the time being. The WordPress site has thousands of templates set up, but you can also just *Google* "free WordPress themes," "inexpensive WordPress themes," or "WordPress themes for businesses," and you will get even more results. Look under handmade, craft, and even your specific product (like soap, candle, custom-made swords, etc.).

Choose a basic theme that you like. Make sure the layout and placement of menus works well for your vision of your site, and then install that theme.

After you get that down, you can start changing icons, buttons, and images. You can customize pages, add the important sections, and manage the site itself. If you're struggling with image manipulation, WordPress itself, or getting things to show up right, there are *hundreds* of free tutorials online, and YouTube is a great help.

But I Don't Have the Patience!

Maybe you don't have the patience to deal with WordPress. Or you just don't have the time or desire to set up your own website, and you're frustrated. I understand. Some of us, no matter how well-intentioned, are not tech-savvy people.

If this is your sticking point, I highly recommend hiring a professional to help you out. Websites like Guru, UpWork, and Fiverr all exist to connect you with people who know what they are doing. Find a freelancer you trust and start the process of allowing *them* to set up your website for you.

Go with someone who fits with your business approach and attitude and seems excited to help you make your business a success. When I work with a freelancer, I find that my best results come when I know exactly what I'm looking for and what I want the final product to look like.

Make sure you have a good idea of how you want your site to be laid out, what you want it to look like, and how you want it to function. Look around on competitor's sites to check out what they're doing right and wrong. Take notes of functions you like and dislike, like complicated menus or difficult navigation.

There's no shame in hiring out the website creation if you simply can't manage it yourself, though I do encourage you to try. If not, bringing in a professional is always a great idea.

HOW TO TAKE PAYMENTS ON A WEBSITE

So you've got a website and you're ready to start selling – but how do you take payments and information? How can you be sure that you always get the orders, and the money, and the shipping information?

Just like your website creation, it's not as complicated as you might think. There are several secure, easy ways to take payment, accept credit cards, and process orders.

PayPal has been the big name for a long time in the internet world, and there's a reason. PayPal is very easy to use once you have an account. You can simply add a "purchase" button on the screen, and PayPal will securely gather the information, including payment information, and send you the money.

Of course, PayPal charges a fee for this service – a percentage of the purchase (in the U.S., PayPal charges businesses and merchants 2.9% per online transaction, plus a small fixed fee). For the US, the fixed fee is currently $0.30. Each currency has a separate fee, however.

This isn't unusual. You're using PayPal's website and their secure servers, so it shouldn't come as a surprise that they want to charge you for that. Each payment processing program, in fact, is going to have some sort of a fee associated with it.

Stripe is an online payment system for small businesses and has a variety of tools to take all sorts of payments, no matter what size your business is. It's relatively fast to set up, it's easy to understand if you have precious e-commerce experience, and it isn't hugely expensive. The fees are about the same as PayPal for most businesses, and don't start getting extreme until you're bringing in over $1 million annually in sales.

In the, *what does Amazon not do* category falls **Checkout by Amazon**. For 2.9%, plus an extra $0.30/transaction fee, you can create a free Amazon account and put a copy-and-paste code on your site. All payments go through Amazon itself, and it's quite easy to use. If you're doing *more* than $3,000 a month in sales, fees go down.

Amazon is a trusted name, and nearly everyone has an Amazon account. If your target market doesn't have a problem with Amazon, this could be a great choice for your business.

Finally, let's tackle another big one: **Shopify** is a bit newer on the scene than other choices like PayPal, but it's become a workhorse for countless small businesses.

Shopify will not only let your customers use their information to check out, but they have dozens of other tools for small businesses as well – like tools to make logos, videos, generate pay stubs, create readable QR codes for your products, generate invoices. Seriously, Shopify offers a lot. You can even generate shipping labels through Shopify with each purchase that is made.

You can choose just to put a point of purchase button through Shopify on your website; or you can use their platform to set up your entire online store, completely hosted on your own domain. This is what *many* small businesses choose, especially when starting out because it's incredibly easy to manage.

Of course, many of these things do have a fee. Just like PayPal, Shopify will cost you. Instead of a percentage of your income going to Shopify (like PayPal does), Shopify charges a flat monthly fee for their services. (That is, if you're using their payment options.) This can range from $30 to $300, depending on your business's needs.

Over 800,000 small and large businesses use Shopify, so it's obviously a useful platform.

What are the cons? If you choose to take payment through PayPal, Stripe, or another non-Shopify payment option, you're going to pay an additional transaction fee on top of that. It can also be a little harder to manage Shopify's options, and they provide less freedom in some ways.

However, for so many companies, the tradeoff is absolutely worth it. Do some research and decide for yourself if it's right for you.

OTHER OPTIONS

As more internet commerce has grown, so have your options. There are hundreds of other online payment platforms out there nowadays: Google Wallet for in-app purchases, Sellfy for digital products, ProPay, BrainTree, PaySimple, Flint, and

Intuit QuickBooks Payment all have a variety of payment processing options.

Facebook Marketplace

Facebook Marketplace is a good, low-cost way of getting your business out there and selling to those local to you. Building a loyal local customer base is key. But rather than offering to meet up, have the person come to your business location. Otherwise, you can spend all afternoon driving around to different drop-off or pick-up zones for a handful of sales. It should be financially worth it to you, and your time matters.

Facebook also has local **community groups** that are great for smaller businesses to advertise or run specials. Most communities have groups that support local or small businesses, so be sure to look into that. Especially during the holidays, you could see a ton of new sales or traffic to your site just because of a comment you make or a post you shared.

Etsy

Depending on what you sell, a website like Etsy might be just the thing to give you some global sales. Do you sell custom t-shirts? Handmade knives? Organic cosmetics or candles or soaps? **Etsy** is a huge marketplace that was started for small artisans looking to sell their crafts and make a living doing something they love.

While Etsy's focus has been handmade, vintage, and craft supplies, it has changed a bit. In recent years, Etsy has seen the growth of drop shipping, mass-produced goods, and more, but there is still space for you.

Selling on Etsy isn't as easy as just throwing a picture on a page and waiting. There are fees and rules to selling on Etsy, so you need to be sure you understand what you're getting into. Every item you list on Etsy has a base listing fee, and every 4 months you need to renew that fee to keep your listing live.

In addition, for every sale you make, Etsy takes a transaction fee. Right now, that fee is 5%, but it does change pretty regularly. Depending on how much product you're selling, this can add up fast.

Is it worth it anyway? For many people, it is.

Most online platforms take some sort of cut, so this really isn't a huge deal. You need to ask yourself if your target market shops on Etsy, and if they would buy your product *on* Etsy. If the answer is yes, an Etsy storefront might be worth it for you.

Selling at Local Stores

Again, depending on your product, you may consider selling it in other stores. For example, if you're an artist, perhaps a local restaurant would let you display your framed work there with a price tag. Perhaps you sell organic cosmetics and someone else sells handmade jewelry—perhaps you could partner in a sense, and each put some product at the other's shop? Collaboration can be a great boost.

If you sell mostly from home or online but have a local artisan gift shop downtown, consider approaching the owner to put your goods on display. This can be a great way to let locals know you exist, and tourists will be able to buy local hand made products for their friends and family as a memento.

In fact, did you know that many Whole Foods grocery stores have a section with locally made products including soaps, candles, lotions, etc.? Why not yours?

There are a lot of things to consider when you're looking at selling through a local retailer or shop, including how much to charge. This is basically a wholesaler situation, so be sure you're making a little bit of profit yourself, but giving the retailer room to make a profit, too. After all, they're managing the overhead, employing staff, and keeping the lights on.

If you're considering approaching a local store, I recommend creating a sample package for the owner or manager of your most popular products. Let them see why your product is different and better than others they might carry. Direct them to your website, but also print them out a price sheet that includes how much you'll charge *them* for it, versus the suggested retail price. Any information about local sales – like, you've sold 350 bars through Facebook Marketplace in the last 12 months – would also do well on this sheet.

Other Local Options

If you're not interested in local stores but you want to sell in person to the local crowd, there are some other options for you. Even if you offer services, local events are a great way to meet new clients from the community. **Farmers' markets, flea markets,** and local **pop-up artisan fairs** are all great options for meeting new local customers. Have flyers with a map to your location, and maybe some coupons to draw them in to your brick-and-mortar later on.

I know a creative real estate agent who goes to the events and meets many potential clients. She allows customers to spin the wheel in exchange for their email, and then she gives them a prize (like a candy bar or a pretty spatula). It's a great way for her to get her business card in their hands and build her email list. Pretty clever.

Of course selling your product is ideal, if you have products that people can purchase right there.

So what can you expect at an event like this? At these outdoor selling events, most of the time you pay a flat rate for a table, and you're responsible for setting up and taking it down. Be prepared. No one is going to help you carry heavy boxes of products or decorate your space. Get there in plenty of time to get a good table, set it up, and display your wares.

It's important that your branding matches your table display. What vibe are you sending? Is it botanical, environmental, all-natural, unique? An old wooden milk crate or small shelves go a long way to making a space feel designed, intentional, and beautiful – all things that will draw people in and make them want to buy from you.

To get a feel for the venue, consider taking a walk through that flea market or bazaar before signing up to see what others are selling and how they are displaying their goods.

Local venues are great to network with other local businesses in your area and make connections you wouldn't normally. Look for other markets where your target demographic shops or find a local artisan shop to connect with. Even just making friends who understand the struggle of a small business can help you stay motivated.

CHAPTER 9 – PROFIT: COMPETITIVE ANALYSIS, CREATIVE PRICING, & FORECASTING

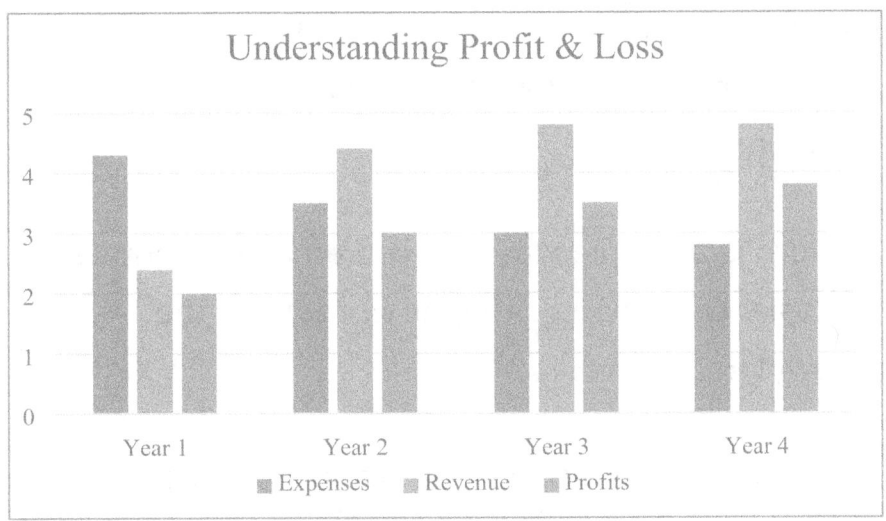

Are you bringing in enough revenue? There could be many reasons for that. In this chapter we will talk about competitive analysis, creative pricing, understanding profit, and business forecasting.

COMPETITIVE ANALYSIS

This is key to having a successful business. When you have a competitive analysis, you know your business's current position within your particular industry.

The competitive analysis allows you to get the information you need on your competitors, market share, market strategies, growth and other important factors. When you have all this information, you will be able to change or improve your business in key areas so you can increase profits and sales.

Here is a simple way you can do a competitive analysis. On a piece of paper write down the following:

1. Number of local competitors you have
2. What their niche is/what products they sell
3. Where they sell
4. What is their pricing

Once you have that list, take a look and see where you would fit in that list, how can you stand out from the crowd, what can you do differently that would make customers pay attention to your products.

In my business experience, I believe there are three ways you can always stand above the crowd. I always have tried to stand above the crowd by trying of these three strategies.

1. By making superior products than my competitors make
2. By offering 100% customer satisfaction guarantee
3. By creative pricing strategy

Let me explain what I mean by creative pricing strategy.

CREATIVE PRICING STRATEGY

Pricing is the most important factor of your business. A carefully thought out pricing strategy can make you very successful, but a pricing strategy that places you above your market can literally put you out of business. On the other hand, pricing below the market can wipe your bottom line profit completely clean; and before you know it, you are out of business and in debt.

So how can you stand out in the crowd without taking dangerous risks? To make yourself more visible among other competitors, you have to be creative when it comes to your pricing strategy. That is where the tricky part comes in. My goal is to teach you how to implement a carefully thought out pricing strategy that can make you stand out, continue to profit, and stay successful.

Here are few ideas I like to try:

1. Always run a monthly special where you offer a discount on one particular product each month, but never the same product for two months in a row.
2. Run a BOGO (Buy One Get One Free) promotion every few months on select products (ones that are not selling well)
3. Never try to be the low price leader. This is a slippery slope; don't reduce your price to stay competitive. It can backfire.
4. Run various package promotions during the holidays. For example, create gift baskets with one or two bags of ground coffee, a box of gourmet cookies, and two decorative mugs all nicely wrapped.

Remember, when it comes to pricing or marketing ideas, there is no "one size fits all." Not every idea works for every business. Some strategies may work better for you than others, and vice versa. So, it is a good idea to test each idea separately and document the results; then analyze and see which one worked the best.

Understanding Profit: Penny Profit, Profit Margin, and Markup

In business, these are three common terms that you may hear or read about, but what do they mean and how they are different from each other? After I started my gas station podcast, I would get emails from time to time about this very topic.

They are not complicated concepts. Let's break them down and see what they are:

Penny Profit

Penny profit is essentially the actual cash profit you make by selling any items in your store. For example, if you sell a bottle of 20 oz. Coke for $1.75, what is the penny profit of that sale?

To find the answer, first we need to see how much you paid for that bottle of Coke. Looking at your invoice from Coke shows that you paid $1.00 for it and sold it for $1.75. So your penny profit is $1.75-

1.00 = 75 cents. Your penny profit is 75 cents. Penny profit is the difference between the selling price vs your actual cost.

Profit Margin

Profit margin the most widely used term in almost every business. It is what we all use to figure out if we are making enough profit from our products and services. Are we making 100% profit? Fifty percent?

Profit margin is essentially the percentage of the profit you make or earn when you sell a product. Confusing? Let's take a look at the same example of that bottle of Coke we used earlier.

We already know the penny profit from that sale was 75 cents. Whether that is a good or bad thing really depends on how much you paid for it. If I paid $5 for it and only made 75 cents, it's not worth stocking on my shelves.

Figuring out the profit margin is done a little differently. To determine the exact margin, we will have to take the penny profit and divide that number by the selling price.

First figure up the penny profit. Then divide that penny profit by the selling price 0.75 divided by $1.75 = 43. We have made a 43% profit margin.

Markup

Let's say that we want to check to ensure we are making least a 50% profit on all of our products. So we want to figure what our markup is. What percentage am I marking up my products from the actual cost that I am paying for them?

To figure out the markup, divide the penny profit by the actual cost. Let's take a look at the same example once again.

Remember that our penny profit from that bottle of Coke was 75 cents. Now we just need to divide that by the actual cost which was $1.00.

Let's do this, 0.75/$1.00 = 75%. This means that we made a 75% markup for that bottle of Coke.

You want to understand these three aspects of pricing so that you can determine if you are making enough of a profit off of all your products. Now, you may offer special deals from time to time to increase foot traffic so that you lower your price on certain products and receive a lower profit temporarily.

But overall you want a strong markup value on everything you are stocking. Otherwise, those things are taking up space on your shelves that might be better served with other more profitable items.

Also, you want to pay attention when your costs go up from your vendors and be able to determine how much you need to increase your prices.

Business Forecasting

This is another valuable business tool if you want to have a profitable business. Business forecasting is essential to determining sales targets.

A month-by-month sales forecast helps you to identify problems and opportunities. An accurate sales forecast along with a well-structured sales plan will help you to have an effective business.

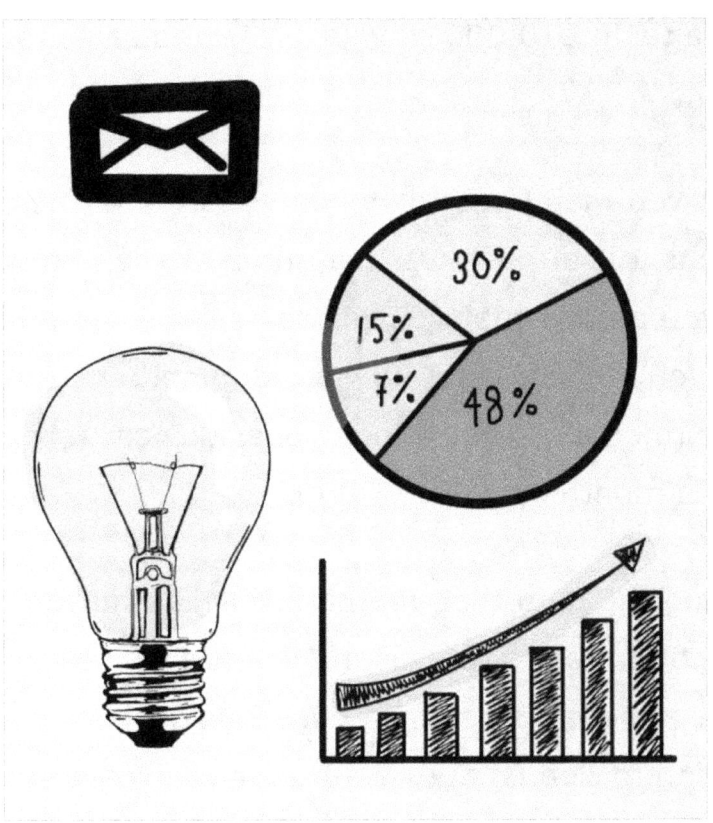

All you need to forecast your business is a little information and an observant eye for trends. Let's say that you want to project your sales for the next three years.

First, look at the sales from the same period last year and compare it to this year. Let's say that last year in this same month, your sales were $100,000. But this year, your sales have been consistently about 10% higher than last year every month. So you can add $10,000 to your projected sales for this month.

But you may need to look at some other factors. Perhaps it is a much warmer summer than normal, and you predict that you will sell even more drinks than you did last year, so you add another 5% to your projection. That brings your business forecast for this month up to $115,000.

Using the data that you had, this is a reasonable projection. Sound forecasting is important for setting attainable goals, creating sound business plans, applying for loans, and reports for your partners.

Chapter 10 – Branding & Marketing

Do people know who you are and what you sell? Do they know why they should buy from you instead of your competition?

We are going to look at *5 Ps* of marketing, then understanding your target market, reaching them, utilizing your physical location, and low-cost, successful marketing.

Then we'll look at branding: Creating a solid brand, telling your story, logo design, and packaging.

In the following chapter, we'll talk exclusively about marketing on social media—because that channel has changed dramatically in the last decade, yet it is one of the most important for small businesses to understand.

THE 5 PS OF MARKETING

1. **Products:** What products do you sell? What are the selling points of your products? Is it nutrition, variety, value? What do you want others to know about the products or services that you offer? This should be one of focal points of your marketing efforts.

2. **Prices:** How much do you charge? Do you offer an exceptional value for your products or services? What is your most competitively priced product? Many businesses will offer a special value or low cost item to draw in business.

3. **Place:** Where do you sell your products or services? Do you have an online store or a brick-and-mortar location? Do you conduct business over the phone? Do you have a website where you sell your products?

4. **Promotion:** How do you spread the word about your products? What marketing channels or mediums do you use to advertise or spread the word about your products or services? Do you have physical signs to draw in foot traffic? Do you advertise on social media, or keep up an active Facebook or Instagram page?

5. **People:** Who are your main customers? How do you connect with them? Do you understand your target market? Who are your employees, or the representatives of your business? Do they understand your goals or the value that you offer the customers?

Your Target Market

Who is your target market, and why are they your target? In other words, who are you trying to sell your products to? People in your area? Other businesses? Those who are willing to pay more for specialty products?

What are they like? What are their buying preferences? Where do they hang out?

It's important to understand who they are before you can answer this question: Are you reaching them? Are you connecting with them? And how can you do a better job of this?

CREATE THE RIGHT IDENTITY.

One way is through branding, creating the right identity for yourself in order to reach your target market. The other of course is by understanding their preferences and offering the products they want to buy. The other way is by making yourself visible to them through advertising and marketing. We will talk about all of these things in this chapter.

This may seem odd to you, but it's a good idea to limit your target market. Think for a moment, who do you want to sell to?

The answer "Everyone!" seems like a smart answer at first, right? Well, no. If your market is too broad, and you try to make everyone happy by being too generic or middle of the road or like everyone else, then you end up appealing to no one at all. As a small, growing business, the only way you can truly compete with 'the big guys' is to target a niche market. The narrower, the better.

Think about it this way: It's better to focus your target on 1,000 people who will likely want to buy your product because it meets their needs, rather than trying to reach 10,000 or even 100,000 who couldn't care less.

Let's take some time, now that you've got some goals aligned, to talk about your target market and who you're selling to. Here are some questions to help you narrow your focus:

- What is the age range of your ideal buyer?

- What does your ideal buyer do for an income?

- What does your ideal buyer like to do in their time off work?

- What education does your ideal buyer have?

- Where does your ideal buyer live? In the US, outside of the US?

- Is your ideal buyer married? Single? Engaged?

- Where is your ideal buyer from?

Think about your product line while you're answering these questions, and form a picture of the perfect buyer and the products that would be perfect for them. How does your product meet their needs? Is there anything you don't carry that they would be interested in?

What do your customers want?

Now, what if you are a brick-and-mortar shop, so you want to appeal to the people who are nearby, or who drive past your business on a regular basis? Think about what they are looking for. What would get them to stop at your shop rather than the other dozen shops or gas stations along their route?

Once I began understanding my target market by listening to my customers and paying attention to their needs, I began to carry the products they wanted. Every time it was a great success.

> LISTENING TO CUSTOMERS WAS A GREAT SUCCESS.

In a rural convenience store, I began selling snacks and refreshments from a certain country for the rural farm workers. At a gas station near a lake, I began selling non-ethanol fuel for boaters. In my sandwich shop near downtown, I began selling the energy drinks that the college students and business persons were requesting.

Every time I listened to my target market and offered what they wanted, I saw a dramatic increase in sales. That's why it's so important for you to identify and understand your target market. And most of the time, they will appreciate it and become your regular customers. Win, win!

What Is Branding?

Have you given careful thought to your brand? Branding is basically how you present yourself to the world. It is essentially your business's identity: Who you are, the core of your business. Have you ever considered how important your name, or your logo, or your website is?

Branding is so very important for small business owners. On your website, and in your pamphlets, and possibly on your labels, you want to share your brand identity. It makes you memorable. It can build customer interest and loyalty.

Brand Identity

First, consider, what's your story? Are you trying to fight poverty by donating a pair of shoes to the needy for every pair you sell? Are you trying to help your customers by offering them free coffee when they fill up on their commute?

As a small business owner, make sure you take into consideration your target market before you settle on brand identity or back story. It should be in line with who you're selling to, and why. If your target market can't connect with your brand, they have no incentive to purchase your products or support you.

Many people like to buy from a business that has the same values or ethics they do. For example, social responsibility, sourcing that protects the environment, a local store that supports the community. What values do you have that they can align with?

Be sure to distance yourself from negativity, discrimination, or anything that could put off your customers. This seems obvious, but it's easy to alienate people without meaning to. So consider your target market and what kind of brand they want to get behind.

You don't need to by phony, and certainly don't be dishonest, but create a brand that is appealing.

If you don't know how to define your story, here are some questions to answer to help you find your brand identity:

Who Are You? Who are you, the owner? Who are you, the brand? As a small business, you aren't just another faceless corporation. Make it clear to your consumers that you are a person who cares about their life, their job, their business, the community, the environment – whatever the case may be.

What Do You Do? What product do you have to sell? What are you making to give to people? Many brands choose to present a "problem" to the consumer and offer the solution they created, effectively being the hero in their own story. Are your products organic, or fair trade, or ethically sourced? Do you offer a better value than most?

Who Do You Do It for? Who is your target market? Who do you want to reach? Who are you trying to help or support with your business? Do you support local sports teams, veterans, and the elderly?

Why Do You Do It? Why Do You Care? This is the section where you show people why you care. Why did you create your company? What drove you to offer this product to your target market? What solutions are you trying to create with this business?

How Do You Do It? What's Your Process? This can be fun, depending on your passion and products. Why did you choose your particular ingredients, how do you craft your candles or beer or specialty coffee? Why does it matter? Are safety and quality important? Talk about it on your website.

What's in the Future? Where do you see yourself and your company in five years? Ten years? Talk about your short- or long-term goals for the company and how you can achieve them. This doesn't have to go as in-depth as your business plan, obviously, but touch on your future with the company. This shows consumers you aren't looking to up and leave; you're here to stay.

Your Logo

Now that you know who you are, you need a **logo.** This is a graphic or picture that goes with your name. When it comes to logos, think carefully about what you want to convey. If you don't have any experience with graphic design or art, I highly recommend hiring out the logo process.

Don't worry: There are countless freelance graphic designers available for a variety of price points, and even a cheap choice is a good investment. Check out sites like **Fiverr.com**, where you can find graphic designers for a very low cost (starting at $5) to do logo design, business and stationary, flyers and brochures, and overall brand style.

Whether you tackle your logo yourself or hire out, have a good idea of what you would ideally want it to look like or convey before you begin. Do you have a color scheme for your brand? Does it match what your target market likes? Do you want a big blocky font, or a curving script?

If you're hiring out, find a few logos that you really love as examples. Note what you like about the logos – the style, the minimalism, the colors, etc. This will help you get a final product you're really happy with, and make your designer's life a lot easier, too.

Your logo should go on as much as possible. Certainly it should be on your website and your sign. But it can also be on your labels, price tags, packaging, boxes or bags.

If you can't afford to have custom-printed cups or bags or boxes, no worries. You can get sheets of colorful stickers and affix them to your packaging or cups. Let's talk about the power of labels:

In fact, your **labels** should have your logo, your name, your website, your address, and your phone number. That way if someone drinks your coffee at their business meeting and wants to hire another round for their department, all they have to do is look at the cup and there is your name and phone number. Again, make it easy for people to find you.

Low-Cost Marketing

What if you could boost sales for free? Or perhaps increase your foot traffic by 10% with a one-time investment of $5 or $25? There are several free or low-cost marketing techniques you can do for your business that will generate interest and visitors.

Business cards should be in your pocket, on your counter tops, posted on local sign boards, etc. These little cards are inexpensive, and yet many people will hold on to them for years.

Blog posts on your website about your process, your tools, or your life can generate interest. Share these on industry sites, crafting sites, business boards, and more.

Flyers or brochures can go in local gathering places, coffee shops, doctor's offices, and more. Print attractive flyers or business cards for yourself, and leave them places your target market hangs out. While this should never be your only way of advertisement, it's a great way to reach a new market that might not spend as much time online.

Be present: Spend some time online where your target market also hangs out. Answer questions on Quora, find communities to promote and share your work on Reddit, and try to build a reputation of a brand people can trust and appreciate.

Don't hesitate to encourage your customers to leave good reviews about your products on social media platforms or other places online. This does nothing but improve your reputation, and gets your name out there.

SHOULD I OFFER DISCOUNTS AND SALES?

Should you offer sales? This is something only you can answer – but many businesses do.

If not sales, consider doing promotional items for holidays like Christmas, Halloween, Thanksgiving, Valentine's Day, Saint Patrick's Day, etc. People tend to spend extra money to celebrate the holidays.

Gift sets for holidays are always a great seller, and if your customers know that you have a changing library of products, then they may return again and again to check out your new products.

If you have a lot of product that you need to move quickly, or you want to boost sales, a sale week can be a great approach.

Be wary of relying on sales for all of your business, though, and make sure you're still making money on each item you sell.

Even though you can sell more in quantity with a deep discount, you might not be able to make the same amount of money.

Remember to consider your profit margin, right?

Offering promotions like frequent buyer cards is a great incentive to draw in repeat customers.

If your incentive is very good, you may also get word of mouth business as they refer their friends. Or you can offer referral discounts or incentives.

LOCATION, VISIBILITY, & STREET TRAFFIC

Is your location a pain point? Let's talk about your store's appearance. Are there any visibility issues there? Any room to improve?

If you have a brick-and-mortar business, I'd like you to take a walk outside. Stand on the sidewalk or in the parking lot, try to see through a consumer's eyes, and ask yourself these questions:

- Is my store clearly visible from the road or sidewalk?

- Is it obvious what I sell or do?
- Is my business's name clearly visible?
- Is the exterior condition of my storefront appealing?
- Do I have any nice-looking promotional signs in the windows?
- What would catch someone's eye and draw them in for a closer look?

Do you see any room for improvement? Although you may have not considered it before, you can do something about each of these questions. In fact, you should!

If it's not obvious what you sell, then you need some pictures or signs. Something recognizable with a quick glimpse. At least in your windows. Make your name larger; invest in a new sign or a low-cost, colorful banner.

If the exterior condition of your storefront leaves something to be desired and you haven't the means to paint the walls or remodel the steps or replace that awning, then you can at least invest in a nice pot of flowers or a bench or a low-cost sandwich board sign.

It's amazing how inexpensive these effective signs are. A simple sandwich board sign that can advertise daily specials to your drive-by traffic is nowadays about $25. If you're hidden behind another business or some trees, one of those large feather banners that waves in the breeze is only about $20. And if your building's sign is outdated, you can cover it with a large colorful banner for only about $10.

If you aren't taking advantage of these types of signs for your brick-and-mortar shop, it really is worth a try.

Your Social Media Presence

Nowadays, your social media presence is everything. Even brick-and-mortar businesses need to promote themselves on social media. In the next chapter, we'll talk about your social media presence: Your page, posts, and advertising for each of the major platforms.

If you have a store or office or business location, do your best to spread the word about your website. Offer coupons in exchange for customer email addresses and so on. Then you can connect to your target market online and build relationships to draw regular customers.

CHAPTER 11 – SOCIAL MEDIA MARKETING

You may be thinking: "Do I need to use social media? I have a brick-and-mortar shop, so is social media really that important for my business?"

Many new business owners ask me this question in one form or another. They tell me how they have a Facebook but never check it. Or they don't 'get' Instagram or Twitter, so they don't bother keeping up with this.

This is probably the single biggest mistake that most of these business owners make, to be honest.

Social media is a *huge* tool used by literally millions upon millions of people each day, and I genuinely cannot overstate how important and helpful strategic social media usage can be for your business.

Here are some statistics for you, if you're not convinced:

- As of 2021, 4.2 billion people use social media.
- The average user spends 145 minutes a day scrolling their SM feeds. That's well over 2 hours each and every day.
- All ages use it: 90% of adults in the US age 18-29. 82% of adults age 30-49, and 69% of adults age 50-64.

There's a good chance that no matter who your target market is, they're using social media - and quite a bit, too.

If you're not utilizing social media for your business, you're missing a huge opportunity for marketing, advertisements, and just getting the word out about who you are and what you can do. Even if you are using social media, then neglecting the platform, not posting regular updates, and not communicating with your user base are all huge mistakes.

Social media is your friend; let's take some time to learn how to use it to your advantage.

Using Facebook for Your Business

Facebook isn't just a social media tool; it has become significant regarding advertising and marketing. Facebook allows businesses to have their own business page and compile data through Facebook Insights. Using this, retailers can compare their social media traffic and enhance their sales.

Facebook is one of the leading websites to promote your store with the help of blogs and brand related information. A retailer must be able to provide valuable information to form a connection and get more shares and likes to position yourself as a favorable brand on Facebook. You can also post questions which are very effective ways to learn what customers want to see in your store, and what they are most likely to purchase. It's like conducting a focus group online, only much easier and efficient as your customers become engaged.

You may have heard that Facebook is starting to become an 'aging' platform, with many of the Gen Z users migrating to other social media platforms like Snapchat or Instagram. But there is still a lot to be said for the social media giant that has nearly 3 billion active users.

Setting up a business Facebook account is easy and fast. Facebook *wants* you to use their platform to promote your business, and they want you to be able to talk to your customers and promote your products. In a very literal sense, your success on their site is also their success. Most of their revenue comes from ads.

Quick FB Tips:

- Make sure your Facebook business page is easy to navigate and that users can quickly find all your important information. Also ensure your page is 'public' in settings.

- Essential information: have your website,

your products, and your contact information.

- Ask a trusted friend or business partner to go through the page and make sure it's easy to use.

- Post live videos on a regular basis, at least one a week. Make them interesting or informative, as well as short and sweet (1 to 3 minutes only). Highlight new or seasonal products, special promotions, or advice.

- Post content that draws in viewers or benefits them in some way. Not every post should be about making a sale. You want to build relationships with your viewers.

- Take surveys; people love them. Ask them to choose their favorite product, or when they like to shop. Think of creative questions. Then use their answers to formulate your next line!

- Hold contests or sales, at your discretion. You know what you can afford and what you have time for. But one rule of social media is that interacting with your viewers will make your page really worthwhile. People may even share it with their friends.

THINK LIKE A CUSTOMER.

As a general rule: Try to think like a viewer or potential customer. What do they need or want to know? I've left many Facebook pages in frustration simply because it wasn't easy to find what I was looking for, like their hours, website, or product information. Make it easy for your potential customers to do business with you.

Using Facebook to Boost Sales

Here is a great idea I tried for my convenience store using Facebook. First create a FB business page for your store, then print out a sign such as this: "Add us as your friend on Facebook and get a $1 off coupon." Then give them your Facebook address or name. Print these up and cut them out, then have an employee pre-stuff them in shopping bags that you use at your store.

When I did this the first time, I gave away about $475 or so the first month from the coupons, but I gained access to that exact number of customers too. The next month, I started to promote some specials on FB that I ran on soda and many other items; I saw my sales increase by about 9% the following month. It works; trust me. Try it and you will be amazed how well this works and how simple this can be.

Remember not to overdo it or forget to do it. Keep it consistent, maybe once a month or so is a great frequency. But if you want to be a little more aggressive, go twice a month.

Should I Use Facebook Ads?

You can also advertise on Facebook. Their ads are so easy to use, and they are really great for narrowing down your target demographic and advertising to only your ideal market.

There are two main ways to utilize Facebook's market and advertisements. The first is to promote your entire business page. This will make your page pop up in a potential customer's feed.

You can select several options: the type of people you want to view your ad (their age, gender, and more); the length of time you want to promote your ad; as well as the amount of money you would like to spend on this particular advertisement campaign. Facebook does the rest – promoting your company's page so that your target market will see it while scrolling through their feed.

You can also promote (boost) a *post*. Let's say you're running a two-week sale on a specific product, and you want as many people to know about it as possible, so you post about it on your Facebook page. You can choose to boost that post, and anyone in your pre-chosen demographic (again, based on the same factors of age, gender, etc.) will see this promoted post about your sale while scrolling. They can click on your name to get to your Facebook page, or any link you have in the post itself, to go directly to your sale landing page.

Like I said, it's very easy to run advertisements on Facebook. The platform makes it as fool-proof as possible to get more views for your page. Be sure you pay close attention to both your budget and your advertisement run-length. It's easy to get carried away when you first start using FB ads and to dump a bunch of money into one or two posts.

Pro tip: Quality is better than frequency, so don't have your posts show up on too many feeds at one time. Make sure that you're only promoting the highest-quality posts that you have, and you're being careful to select your target market.

USING INSTAGRAM FOR YOUR BUSINESS

At the end of 2020, it was estimated there were 1.16 billion Instagram users, with 500 million daily user stories. That's a *ton*. So if you're skipping Instagram, you're missing out on all of these people actively using this growing platform.

Just like with Facebook, Instagram makes it very easy to create a business account and get started. Once you have your account set up, you can connect Instagram and Facebook. So if you choose to make a post on Instagram, it will automatically show up on Facebook, too.

Pro tip: I don't recommend doing this *all the time*, but the occasional cross-post is fine. Ideally, your customer who loves your product is going to follow you on all of your platforms, and seeing the same post with the exact same wording on both Facebook and Instagram will get old fast. Make sure you change it around, at least a little, to keep it fresh and interesting to read.

Tip: Links in Instagram

One thing to know about Instagram is that, unlike Facebook, you *cannot* add links to the bottom of your posts. There is zero outbound linking on Instagram. The only place you can add a link is in your bio, and there are a few ways to handle this. You can just put your website in your bio, or you can use the most popular option, 'Link in Bio'.

A **link in bio** tool basically lets you put a corresponding link in each new post you have. So if you want to post a photo of a specific product or a sale page, you can link *directly* to that in your bio instead of just sending your users to the full website and making them figure out where to find it.

There are several programs that let you do this, including Lnk.Bio, LinkTree, Tap.Bio, and Shorby. Choose the one that's easiest for *you* to use and manage, and what you think looks the best. If you're a little lost, I recommend checking out a few competitor's social media pages to see what tool they use and if you like the way it looks to a potential consumer.

Unlike Facebook, hashtags are a big thing on Instagram. If you use a hashtag, it shows up in a search for that hashtag. So if you use the hashtag #handmadesoap, anyone searching Instagram for that hashtag can find your post. They can also click on that hashtag and see all the posts with it.

The 'ideal' number of hashtags for a post is between 7 and 30, according to recent marketing studies. This is a really big number, so I'm going to recommend you use as many as makes sense without going overboard. Again, check out what your competitors are doing. How many hashtags are they using? What hashtags?

You should have a few 'core' hashtags that describe your product, and branch out from there depending on what you are posting about. I also personally recommend using a hashtag that is in line with your brand – so, if your business name is "Mrs. Bee's Best Honey," the hashtag #mrsbeesbesthoney should be on each and every post. Encourage happy customers not only to tag you, but to use your hashtag as well.

How Do I Choose Hashtags?

Instagram makes it *super easy* to find hashtags that are used a lot. Open up Instagram on your computer, and start typing in a hashtag you want to use. Let's try #handmadesoap for example.

The hashtag itself has 2.2 million posts. Also, #handmadesoaps, a variant, has over 405,000. The hashtag #handmade has over 255 million.

Just typing in #soap brings up over 8 million posts tagged that way; #soapmaking has nearly 1.5 million, and #soapmaker has over 685,000 posts.

If the hashtag you're using has a lot of posts, that means it's popular, *obviously*. Though it also means it has more competition, so that's something to keep in mind. If too many people are also using that hashtag, your post can also get drowned out.

I find a combination of very popular and somewhat popular hashtags work best. Think about the picture, the format, and what you're promoting or talking about. Ideas to try: #selfcare, #selfcaretips, and hashtags with the soap's scent notes are all great choices.

Should I Use Instagram Ads?

My short answer: Probably!

Much like Facebook, Instagram will let you promote your posts and spend money to gain more viewers. You can choose the amount of time your ad campaign runs for, the target demographic you want to see your ad, and then you let it go and see how it does.

Just like with Facebook, be careful of going crazy or overspending on just one or two posts. Be sure each post that you promote is well designed, well written, and a good example of your branding and your product. Otherwise, you're just cheapening your brand, and no one is going to be interested. Certainly *not* the goal.

In addition to adding a promotion to your posts, you can also promote your *stories*. Your Instagram stories are kept in that little bar up top when you open up the mobile app. Stories are basically short 'snippets,' either just an image (with text overtop) or a video. Story ads are a great way to promote your product and your brand, and your ad will take up their whole mobile screen. No distractions, no other posts, just you and your business, front and center.

The Facebook Ad manager handles all Instagram ads as well, so everything will be kept in one place, nice and organized.

Using Pinterest for Your Business

Pinterest is a little more complicated of a platform, but with over 450 million active users, Pinterest could still be well worth it for you. Take a moment before dedicating a lot of time to Pinterest to think about your target market – do they use Pinterest a lot? Is it a common platform for them to find ideas, products, and more?

I find that despite how popular Pinterest is, not a lot of people necessarily reach for the platform *first* for their social media usage or ads.

Pinterest quick facts to keep in mind:

- Pinterest is the 4th most popular social media platform, behind YouTube, Facebook, and Instagram. It is used more than Twitter, Snapchat, and LinkedIn.
- 77% of Pinterest's user base is women.
- Nearly 8 out of 10 mothers use Pinterest. So if your target market includes moms, there is a good chance they are using Pinterest.
- 34% of people aged 18-29 used Pinterest in 2019. 35% of those aged 30-49 used it.
- 60% of Pinterest users search for a product through the platform to find ideas on what to buy.

- Each Pinterest post has a longer lifespan than Facebook or Instagram. A pinned post can have as long as a 3-month impact on the site, while Facebook has a short organic life span of just a few hours, and Instagram of 48 hours.

Convinced?

If your target demographic is using Pinterest, *so should you*.

Starting a Pinterest business account is very easy, and Pinterest walks you through how to add your website, describe your business, and connect your other social media accounts – including your Etsy page if you choose to sell on Etsy.

Getting Started on Pinterest

Pinterest is all about pictures! So the first thing you should do is go into your settings and set a profile picture – of yourself, your brand, whatever represents your business. The ideal dimensions are 165x165 pixels (px).

Then, go into the *About Your Profile* section and fill that out. You don't need a lot, but do describe your company and use some keywords that describe your brand properly, like *organic, natural, handmade,* etc. Remember the words that you wrote in your word cloud in the branding section? That's a good jumping-off point.

Pro Tip: Under "Account Settings" is one called "Claim." Make sure you fill that out so that all of your associated accounts are claimed to you, including your website. This lets you track website analytics (Who is going from Pinterest to your site? How much traffic has Pinterest generated for you?). Also, any pins that link *back* to your claimed accounts include both a follow button *and* your chosen profile picture.

How to Create Good Pins

Creating a good *pin* (which is a post on Pinterest) isn't hard, but you should put some time into it. Photos should be high quality, clear, and even customized to Pinterest with borders or information. Making your pin stand out from the crowd and catch someone's eye should be the first priority.

Square pins should be 1000x1000px, but it's recommended that you use Pinterest-style pin images, which are 1000x1500px. A 2:3 aspect ratio is the sweet spot, so people scrolling through their feed on their phones can see the full image clearly.

Give it a title, a short description, and then add your destination link. The title should be short, sweet, and descriptive. The description can be a little longer, and make sure you're using *searchable* terms and keywords that describe your products and your business (like soap, handmade, lavender, coconut oil, etc.).

Just remember that simply pinning a plain image won't go far in helping people find you.

How to create a new pin: To upload an image as a pin, click the bottom right + sign, and choose Upload a Pin. Choose Image. Then add the URL and description. Pick a board for your pin, then click Save.

Pro Tip: Go to a competitor's Pinterest account and poke around a little. How are their pins organized? What boards do they have? What are some keywords they use to help people find their pins?

This is called market research: See what is working for other people. Don't plagiarize, but do gain inspiration.

Do I use hashtags on Pinterest posts?

Oh, the age-old debate: Do you use hashtags on Pinterest like you do on Instagram? The answer ranges from no to maybe to not really. Confused? It seems like everyone is.

Unlike Facebook and Instagram, which heavily encourage users to promote posts and also explain how their algorithm works – or Twitter, which encourages you to use hashtags – it's a lot harder to determine how Pinterest's search system actually functions. This is frustrating for a lot of people, not just small business owners. And it seems like every time someone nails down a system, they change it.

Pinterest's official word lately is that hashtags don't really do much for you. When Pinterest first gained popularity, hashtags worked like Instagram in that you could find popular ones, search by hashtags, and more. They have since changed their algorithm to move away from hashtags. Instead, it seems that it looks for keywords within the post and ties that to searches.

In my opinion? No, ditch the hashtags, but do keep keywords and searchable terms in your posts. However, if you want to use hashtags in your descriptions, technically, they still work on mobile but not for desktop. So I would advise you to use strong keywords.

Should I Use Pinterest Ads?

Once again, just like with Facebook and Instagram, using ads on Pinterest is very easy. Choose your best pin or the pin you want the most people to see, and fill out all the necessary information, including campaign duration, market, and more.

These will show up as users scroll through their feed on Pinterest or search for specific things (keywords, like *handmade lotion*).

Pinterest ads can be very powerful, so if your target demographic uses the platform a lot, this can be a great way to really narrow your focus and target the people you want to sell to most.

USING TWITTER FOR YOUR BUSINESS

While Twitter is *less* used as a marketing tool for a business like yours, it can – and should – still be utilized to drive traffic and keep existing customers engaged. Just like with every other platform, Twitter makes it super easy to set up a business account and start posting, commenting, and sharing.

Choose a handle that ideally is your brand name. If your company name is Baskets by Jane, @BasketsByJane should be your handle. However, with millions of users, that name *might* be taken. In that case, try to pick a name that is relevant, like @GetBasketsByJane, @BuyBasketsByJane, or even something like @UseBasketsByJane.

Make sure your profile stands out: Spend time customizing your account. Make sure your logo and your banner image are high quality. Describe your brand well, and make it easy to read and see. Your user icon should be your logo or a very identifiable image.

If you want to get creative, you can have some fun with your banner – adding colors, designs, or even changing it out seasonally if that is something that you enjoy.

You can choose to pin a post on Twitter, and that post will *always* be on top. Choose one that represents your brand, your ideals, or your products.

You can also change out your pinned post at any time, so if you're running a sale or promotion, that would be a great place for it. Make sure that your pinned post is *always relevant*. There is nothing less appealing to me than opening up a business's social media account and seeing an outdated pinned post about an old sale, promotion, or something seasonal that is out of date.

Hashtags on Twitter

Hashtags are used on Twitter in a similar way to Instagram. You can find ideas, share similar concepts, and more. *However*, unlike Instagram, Twitter has a set character count, and you really shouldn't be overloading your posts with hashtags. One or two relevant, important hashtags are the best choice.

Be careful trying to jump on a 'bandwagon' hashtag, or something very high trending, just to get views. It might work in the short term, but make sure you are not misrepresenting yourself or your brand. If your tweets aren't contributing to your brand or your company or benefiting your customers, they shouldn't exist.

Should I Use Twitter Ads?

On Twitter, tweet chats allow a retailer to engage the customers and show them that they are interested in listening to their opinions. It can also help identify influencers and engage with them. Tweet chats can also help gather consumer insights.

It could be used as an effective way to gather data by conducting a poll, engaging in trending conversations, and position your brand as favorable. Twitter can also be used to entice customers, engage in friendly jokes, and talk about products in a funny way to generate buzz.

Just like every other social media platform, you can advertise on Twitter. It's pretty straightforward, and it's very beginner-friendly. The main promotion tool you're going to use is called a promoted tweet.

A promoted tweet is just like a promoted post on another platform, and it shows up on a user's feed while they are scrolling around. You can choose the audience you want to target and how long you want to run that campaign, just like with Instagram or Facebook.

Promoted tweets are just like regular tweets, except they show up in a feed because you paid for them. This means that users can comment on and retweet your promoted tweet. You set your budget based on how many views, and Twitter will never charge you more than what you're willing to spend.

How Often Should I Post?

I recommend at least one post a day for the main social media accounts, like Twitter, Facebook, and Instagram. For Pinterest, you can probably get away with three times a week. Over 90% of businesses post once or more per day, so one post a week isn't really going to cut it.

Find a good balance by posting an appropriate amount, and not overwhelming your customer base and blowing up their feed. I recommend 1 standard post a day for social media, plus 1-2 story posts for Instagram and Facebook to start. As you see engagement and figure out what is working best for your market and your brand, you can increase this number.

You obviously do not need to promote every single post that you do; in fact, I recommend that you don't. It will get expensive quickly, and it's really not financially worth it to shove your product in your target market's face *so* aggressively.

Only choose your best or most relevant posts to promote, and don't have so many campaigns running at once that you can't keep track of everything. You want to learn as you go to see what is most effective.

Overwhelmed by Posting?

This number can be intimidating to users, and I get it. If you don't want to physically log in and make a new post every single day, I *highly* recommend scheduling posts out a week in advance.

As long as it's not a time-sensitive post, you can schedule posts far in advance using a scheduling tool. There are *dozens* out there, so find one that fits your budget and your needs. Tailwind is great for Pinterest, while Sendible can be awesome for Facebook and Twitter. Use what you're most comfortable with, or ask creator friends what *they* use to schedule and keep track of their posts.

I like scheduling posts ahead of time. Once a week – usually Friday or Monday – I will sit down and figure out what I want to post for the whole week. I'll spend a small chunk of time that day, and then I can forget about posting for the rest of the week.

If you do use a scheduling tool, I recommend one that shows you analytics, too.

Analytics help you find out when your customers are viewing your posts most and engaging the most, so that you continue to post in those time slots. Maybe the lunch hour is getting a lot of attention, or the time after dinner but before bed. Maybe your customers see you in the morning, while they are are getting up and just starting their day.

WHAT TO POST ON SOCIAL MEDIA

This is a common concern for people when they first start posting and sharing to their social media: *What should I be posting?*

I recommend finding a balance between sales-focused posts – "Look at this product! I'm featuring this thing! Check out my site!" – and posts with engaging, interesting content. If you *only* post hard sales posts, your consumers are going to be turned off. Sprinkle in a funny meme about candle making, facts about why hand-made candles are so much better than commercially made products, interesting facts about candle making, aromatherapy, and more.

Before you publish your post, ask yourself:

- Is this post relevant to the customer?
- Is it interesting/engaging/helpful?
- Is this well written? Are there typos or grammatical mistakes?
- Does this fit my target audience?
- Does this fit my brand?

If the answer is 'no' for any of those questions, revise your post until you reach that 'yes.' While perfection is the enemy of production, remember that you're running a business. You can post whatever you feel like to your personal account. But your business social media account? A totally different story.

Social media is not just for posting products, interesting facts, or things worth noting. Social media is also the perfect platform to engage your customers.

Social media is one of the best ways to interact. Open the channels of communication with customers and give them a feel for your brand. It helps nurture relationships with customers which otherwise could be difficult to do on an ongoing basis such as in a brick-and-mortar store. If you're not online and only operating from a store using traditional marketing, it does not give you the opportunity to engage in meaningful communication with the customer.

So what should you do on social media to foster a strong relationship with customers?

Talk to them. Respond to comments on your posts, answer questions, and start discussions. The intimate interactions you get on social media are hard to replicate in other places, and it's so important that you're identifying with your market and creating a human persona behind the business.

People will go back to a small business again and again not just for a great product, *but for a great owner.* Always remember this in your interactions.

Taking to social media to deal with customer issues is also a great choice. If you have a customer who is unhappy with their product or purchase in general, encouraging them to message you through social media instead of your email gives them a personal, direct feel. It reminds them that they are dealing with a real person, not just a faceless corporation, and you'll able to respond much faster than you would otherwise.

In short? Talk to your customers online. Build customer loyalty, encourage discussion, respond to their posts on your page and any comments. Keep engaging your customers, and they will keep coming back for more.

Utilizing Email

Remember my great idea about using coupons to get customers on my business Facebook page? You can do virtually the same thing with email.

Have a sign-up sheet or small individual sheets at the counter where customers can give you their name and email address in exchange for a discount or a reward. "Sign up for monthly special discounts" etc.

Ask your employees to have customers fill them out and keep the emails in a safe place.

I assure you that in just two weeks you could have over 300 names in your email list that you can directly market to.

One word of advice: Don't overdo it; do not send them an email every week or every day, but only when you have some real savings and promotions for them. I would say send a truly valuable email once a month.

To keep them from blocking you or marking you as spam, you need to do a few things: Remind them in the email that they signed up to receive it: *Thank you for signing up for my special monthly discount email.*

And be sure to have a button at the bottom or instructions to allow them to unsubscribe at any time. This is important to keep you from being blocked by the email servers.

What kinds of specials should you send? For example, your 2-liter sodas are going on sale next week for a whole month; send them an email notifying them of that sale along with two other sales. Try to have at least three different sales in one email, and try to send one every month. Again, not every week.

Now let's talk about how to send these emails. There are a couple of email marketing companies that you can sign up with, and if you have less than one thousand subscribers, you can use them for free, meaning absolutely no cost to you.

One way is MailChimp; I personally use their service, and it is free. Go to mailchimp.com and sign up for a free account and then take their guided video tour and see how simple it is to send hundreds or even thousands of people one email just by clicking a button. Make your promotions valuable to your customers, and it will be a win-win!

CHAPTER 12 – STAYING MOTIVATED

This final chapter offers you practical ways to stay motivated. I want to provide some real help, resources, and final advice to benefit you and your small business.

First let me ask you, what is draining your energy? What is dulling your passion? What has got you discouraged? Really try to identify what the source of that is, and then take some of the steps in this chapter for help. Don't just force yourself to push on through; try to identify and solve the problem.

Why? Because it's so important for you to stay motivated. As a small business owner, so much is resting on your shoulders. You are the one who provides the vision, who steers the ship, who can make positive change for growth. If you're suffering or burnt out or feeling discouraged, then your business is going to suffer. But there are steps you can take to get to a better place.

> IF YOU'RE BURNT OUT, YOUR BUSINESS IS GOING TO SUFFER.

We'll talk about a few key things that small business owners struggle with and how to find help.

FREE RESOURCES, HELP, & ADVICE

First of all, did you know there are entire communities out there designed to assist small business owners like yourself?

Many times—whether you're a new business owner or an old hand at business—you will encounter something that leaves you at a loss. You're not sure what to do or where to go from here. If you need advice on how to solve a problem or increase business, there are plenty of small business associations and groups to supply answers, advice, and tools to grow your business.

Connecting with like-minded entrepreneurs opens up realms of possibilities: giving you access to a wealth of small business knowledge and experience, supplying advice and inspiration for your company. If you'd like to learn new skills or grow your business, try joining a small business association.

Here is a list of some of the top ones. You can easily find them online and learn what they are all about:

7 Small Business Associations

1. Small Business Administration Community Groups

Did you know that the SBA has regional and district offices that offer a variety of business resources and advice? You can meet other business owners, take classes, learn about financing, or find new business opportunities. SBA community group in your area is a great place to start. (They also have special offerings for women, minority, and veteran small business owners). *Sba.gov*

2. **SCORE**

According to their website: "SCORE's mission is to foster vibrant small business communities through mentoring and education. With the nation's largest network of volunteer, expert business mentors, SCORE has helped more than 11 million entrepreneurs since 1964." This free national network of business mentors works with small business owners to help them develop and grow in a lot of different areas. While you're on the website, check out the "Resilience Hub"—it offers training and business-related courses, resources like webinars, and mentoring.

According to SCORE, business owners who received 3+ hours of mentorship reported higher revenues and increased growth. So no matter the type of business you run, SCORE may help bring you to the next level. *Score.org*

3. Local Chamber of Commerce

If you target a small local market, consider joining your area chamber of commerce. If you sell B2B, you could find customers through chamber events, and you'll have access to professional development resources like workshops, newsletters, and local events.

4. NFIB

The National Federation of Independent Business advocates for almost 350,000 small business members at the state and local level. They try to encourage policies that are in the best interests of small businesses. They also offer discounts, events, online forums, etc. They host networking events and SB research. Nfib.com

5. BNI

Although you have to be approved to join, you could be the voice of your industry in your local area at networking events and meetups. Members also receive benefits workshops, newsletters, and trade show opportunities. Bni.com

6. Meetup.com

While this is technically a social media platform, there is a section dedicated to small businesses. You can use it to meet other business people like yourself to share ideas, get advice, and find customers or partners locally. Meetup.com

7. Industry and Trade Associations

Do some research into associations or trade groups in your specific industry. For example, the National Restaurant Association (restaurant.org) offers advocacy, workforce development, education, networking, and discounts.

The Coin Laundry Association (coinlaundry.org) has been around since 1960 and offers owners help with marketing, education, advocacy and insurance, and selling their business. They even have webinars and events. Who knew?

IMPORTANT ISSUES

Work/Life Balance

So often we work hard to be a good provider for our families. But if we sacrifice spending time with them along the way, then we are depriving them of something more valuable than money: ourselves. Be careful not to sacrifice too much family time for the sake of your business. It's so easy to do when you are running a small business.

Also, we need to take care of ourselves. If we never stop to enjoy the fruits of our labor, why are we working so hard? There is a time to work, and a time to rest. To truly rest, we need to relax to the point of forgetting about the business. Go hiking, golfing, fishing, window-shopping. Take a friend out to lunch and don't talk about the business at all. It will keep your head clear and your life balance.

Finally, be sure to look after your health: eat well, exercise when you can, and make sure you are getting good sleep. While you can function on 5-6 hours of sleep a night, you won't be at the top of your game. And instead of helping your business, it could suffer. Think long-term and stay balanced.

Focus/Looking Ahead

Have you lost focus? Do you feel like you're drowning in the daily grind? Let me ask, what motivates you? What kinds of goals mean something to you? Maybe building up your retirement account, taking on another business venture, or starting a new product line?

Keeping an eye on the future is a good way to stay motivated. Remember your SMART goals? Shoot for something specific, realistic, and attainable.

Then when you reach your goals, stop and celebrate. Looking ahead and reaching small goals will help you stay motivated.

Remember to Outsource

Are you overwhelmed? Maybe you're doing too much yourself. It's a common problem with small business owners who built their company from scratch. It's your baby. You know all of the pieces. You want it done right. I understand. But you are only one person.

Are you doing the work of three or five people? Are you carrying most of the load yourself? Let me gently encouraged you to outsource some of that work. Of course being familiar with each role in your company isn't a bad idea; that way, you'll know better how to train your employees and what common problems arise with each role.

However, as your business grows, you must outsource some of your work in order to expand your business and to avoid burnout.

What can you outsource? Anything you won't be able to prioritize as you grow. That can include sales, marketing, accounting, research, and even manufacturing, shipping, and more.

Even if you can't hire someone full-time at 40 hours a week, getting a freelancer to do 5-10 hours a week of work for you could free up your plate and help you continue to grow.

If this book has helped you in any way, I would love to hear from you. I have been a small business owner for more than 35 years, and I care about your success as a fellow business owner. Please leave me a **review** wherever you purchased my book; it would mean a lot to me.

Feel free to reach out to me either via my blog or through our Facebook group, you can always email me at Shabbir@GasStationBusiness101.com.

All the best,

Shabbir

www.ingramcontent.com/pod-product-compliance
Lightning Source LLC
Chambersburg PA
CBHW052309220526
45472CB00001B/48